POWER
A N D
INFLUENCE

Mastering the Art of Persuasion

Robert L. Dilenschneider

President and Chief Executive Officer
Hill and Knowlton, Inc.

PRENTICE
HALL
PRESS

New York   London   Toronto   Sydney   Tokyo   Singapore

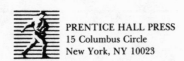

PRENTICE HALL PRESS
15 Columbus Circle
New York, NY 10023

PRENTICE HALL PRESS and colophons are registered trademarks
of Simon & Schuster, Inc.

Library of Congress Cataloging-in-Publication Data
Dilenschneider, Robert L.
   Power and influence : mastering the art of persuasion / by
Robert L. Dilenschneider. — 1st Prentice Hall Press ed.
     p.   cm.
   ISBN 0-13-464041-1 : $19.95
   1. Public relations.   2. Persuasion (Psychology)   3. Public
relations consultants—Professional ethics.   I. Title.
HD59.D56   1990
659.2—dc20   89-70920
                                      CIP

Designed by Richard Oriolo

Manufactured in the United States of America

10 9 8 7 6 5 4 3 2 1

First Edition

This book is for
Geoffrey and Peter
who should know and refine
the points that follow

Acknowledgment

Ron Beyma, who is a communications counselor in Europe and the United States, helped to conceptualize this book. I want to thank him for his valued contribution.

Contents

Introduction   xi

Part I

RECOGNIZING THE
INFLUENTIAL MANAGER

1. The Power Triangle   3
2. The Favor Bank   11
3. Tough Managers and Temperamental Managers   19
4. Image Quacks   25
5. Influence and Integrity   31
6. The CEO's Circle   43

Part II

BECOMING THE
INFLUENTIAL MANAGER

7. The First 100 Days   51
8. The New—and More Influential—You   59
9. What to Do When the Trick Is on You   69
10. Use Your Symbolic Role   77
11. How to Read the *Wall Street Journal*
    in Three Minutes   87

Part III

INFLUENCING
THE MARKETPLACE

12. Intelligence Gathering   95
13. Research—Debriefing the Marketplace   107

CONTENTS

14. The Need for Bad Guys—and Good Guys   117
15. The Attack Agenda   127
16. The Defense Agenda   137

Part IV

IN TIMES OF CRISIS

17. Marathon Repels Mobil   151
18. The Kansas City Hyatt Disaster   159
19. Three-Mile Island: The Noncrisis   165

Part V

THE POWER OF THE MEDIA

20. Hot Type and NASA Mobs   173
21. How to Look at Reporters . . . and Get Them to
    Run Your Story   185
22. Rumors and Leaks, Releases and Pix   199
23. Television and the Electronic Agenda   209

Part VI

UNDERSTANDING THE GOVERNMENT
AND THE SPECIAL INTERESTS

24. Playing the Iron Triangle   217
25. The General Rules of Special Interests   227
26. Labor Today   239

Conclusion   243

Notes   251

Index   253

Introduction

In my business, bad news almost always comes on a week-end, and Saturday, March 2, 1989, was no exception. Shortly after 9:00 P.M. the phone rang in our Fifth Avenue Manhattan apartment. As I got up to answer, my wife's glance at me suggested curiosity mixed with sympathy.

The caller was a lawyer from Philadelphia who said he needed "the best PR firm in the country" to help the Chilean government face a terrible crisis.

Their problem? The safety of Chilean fruit was being challenged by the U.S. Food and Drug Administration. An FDA inspector in Philadelphia, acting on an anonymous tip, had made a special examination of a tiny portion of the hundreds of thousands of tons of Chilean fruit that are exported to the United States every day, and he found two contaminated grapes: two grapes out of 600,000 crates of fruit.

Nonetheless, lab tests indicated that the grapes had been injected with cyanide, a most deadly poison. The news was already out, and the American public was going to be horri-fied. FDA Commissioner Frank Young was about to go on television and ban the sale of Chilean grapes.

"Can Hill and Knowlton help?" asked my caller.

"Of course," I said, and began to make arrangements for an immediate meeting.

Over the next days and weeks, we did an enormous amount of work with the FDA. We monitored the press in better than one hundred cities around the world around the clock and prepared reports every six hours. Coordinating our efforts with the Chilean decision makers in Washington, New York, and Philadelphia, we made sure that the Chileans were able to present a single consistent position to the Commerce Department, the Federal Trade Commission, and the FDA. We also reinforced with the FDA the risk of inappropriately submitting to terrorist demands. We finally convinced the FDA that the real villains in the piece were unknown, and that there had been two victims: the American consuming public and the fruit growers of Chile. The identity of the villain, or villains, was never learned, but it could have been someone from one of several camps, a rival grape grower who also operated on a global scale, a banker stung by a bad Chilean loan, or even a political enemy of Chile's President Augusto Pinochet.

The point, however, was not who did it but was the danger to the consuming public real? Fortunately, it was not: No other contaminated grapes were ever found. So our job was to convince the FDA to lift its ban on the Chilean fruit, and this we were able to do.

How did we do it? We broadened the field. By that I mean we went to the FDA and said, in effect, "Are you really going to punish the Chileans because you found two grapes in 600,000 cases?"

The industry and the consumer shouldn't be penalized for that. So, by our persistence, we got the FDA to come out and say the grapes were okay. Next we got the trade and the media to recognize that the grapes were okay—and we got the message across to the media of the entire country, not just to the East Coast.

So we broadened the field of information by including the trade, the industry, consumers, the media—and then we demonstrated to them the absurdity of being bamboozled by two grapes in 600,000 crates of fruit.

Just before the grape scare hit, there had been another near-panic involving fresh fruit. This one had to do with the effects of Alar, a chemical used by apple growers, that was suspected of being carcinogenic to children. I'm sure that if the Alar scare hadn't come just before the discovery of the two contaminated grapes, the public—and the U.S. government—would never have had such an extreme reaction.

To its credit, once the public realized that someone had been trying to manipulate it by challenging the safety of fresh fruit, it reacted by dismissing the threat from its collective mind, and the whole issue disappeared rapidly.

We were careful, however, never to try to dismiss the public's fear directly. When the scare was over, the *Wall Street Journal* editorialized on the grape and apple scares: "Public officials have learned that standing up to the howling of activist groups, politicians and melodramatic TV reports is like trying to resist the mob storming Frankenstein's castle. As a defense, officials hide behind zero-risk absolutism," which simply means that managers won't take risks that would compromise their job, their department, or the person who put them in the job!

As inherently wrong as a zero-risk approach may be, it nonetheless remains a very widespread reaction. The tendency on the part of top corporate executives to use it is deeply ingrained. But it is, in every instance I can think of, the wrong reaction.

What you have to do, especially if you are dealing with an unsafe product situation, is to take a deep breath and then see if the panic is warranted. If it isn't then you can isolate the fear, step by methodical step, and counteract it.

———

Another time the call came on a Sunday night. It was in February 1982, and the voice on the other end of the line was that of Dean McGee, of the mammoth Kerr-McGee Company. Truly a statesman of the energy industry, Dean was calling about the latest in a series of public relations crises that had been plaguing Kerr-McGee since the 1974 death of Karen Silkwood, a young woman who had worked in one of the company's plutonium plants. This crisis involved an about-to-be-released movie version of Silkwood's life that starred Meryl Streep, Kurt Russell, and Cher.

"Mr. Dilenschneider," he said, in a quintessentially no-nonsense voice, "I'm told you're the best public relations man in the country. My board is very upset about this movie, and our Wall Street people tell us we must *do* something. If you agree to tackle the problem, I'm authorized to offer you one million dollars."

"Thanks for the compliment and the offer," I said, "but I'll need to check into the matter and think about it awhile before I can give you an answer. I'll call you back in a few days."

Silkwood had been a plutonium plant employee who claimed she'd been exposed to dangerous levels of radiation because of unsafe conditions in the Kerr-McGee plant near Crescent, Oklahoma; in fact, she had testified to that effect before the Atomic Energy Commission.

On November 13, 1974, while driving to meet a *New York Times* reporter, the twenty-seven-year-old woman had a fatal auto accident. The autopsy found traces of a tranquil-izer and some alcohol in her blood, which suggested she had fallen asleep at the wheel, but some people, in particular antinuclear people, alleged foul play. Despite the fact that Kerr-McGee was later able to show that its plant had been operating in compliance with federal safety standards, in certain circles Silkwood was revered as an antiestablishment martyr.

Now the movie was coming out, and Dean McGee and his people feared it would perpetuate that image unjustifiably, further damaging their company.

Two days after Mr. McGee's call, I called him back. "I'm prepared to tackle your problem," I said, "but it's not going to cost you a million. It's only going to cost $5,000."

"What do you mean?" he asked incredulously.

I said, "I've thought quite a bit about this, and talked with a lot of my colleagues. And I've done some 'soft soundings' with opinion leaders and a few carefully selected editors. All done, of course, in a subtle way that would not identify you or your problem. The number of people *who can affect your business and your profitability* and who will (a) see this film and (b) be troubled by it is very small. The way I figure it, the number of people you have to influence with your side of the story is about thirty, all of them basically security analysts. And I will help you find a way to influence those thirty people."

Dean McGee said nothing, so I continued. "You don't have to influence the general public. And even if you wanted to, there's no efficient way to do so. What you have to realize is that the movie is going to be around for years: first in the theaters, then on home video, cable, network, and syndicated TV. Accepting that is the first thing you have to do; the second thing is to ignore it.

"The reason no one else matters is because you don't have a product like Cheerios. You sell to the trade. It's not as if Kerr-McGee has service stations, or sells directly to people's homes. You're selling the *middleman*, and we can help make sure that your middleman relationship remains solid."

Dean McGee agreed, though not without a certain degree of skepticism, to try our plan. So we went ahead and contacted those thirty key analysts and industry observers, and gave them, in essence, the same explanation we'd given him. Just as we'd predicted, the problem went away. And our bill to Kerr-McGee was *less* than $5,000.

A couple of months later, the company came back to us. They said they felt they ought to do something to reassure their own employees that they were not corporate bad guys. We liked the idea, and suggested they place some institutional ads in their home state of Oklahoma. The ad campaign, which depicted the strong community participation of the Kerr-McGee employees in such worthwhile organizations as the Boy Scouts, the Community Chest, the Red Cross, and the United Way, gave the company's employees a renewed sense of pride. It also gave them evidence of their company's humanity, which they, in turn, could use to educate people who saw only the Hollywood version of the story.

When we got the initial call from Dean McGee we could have just gone ahead. We could have just begun gathering intelligence on the nature and severity of the problem and run up a huge bill, on the assumption that a massive expenditure was necessary in order to fix things. The client had already offered a million dollars, and would probably have been perfectly willing to spend more.

We could have assumed that because the issue had broad visibility, we would *have to* spend a bushelbasket of money. Not so. In fact, had we done so, we would have magnified the problem, and still failed to reach, and influence, the audience that mattered: the people whose misperceptions of the Silkwood affair could have hurt Kerr-McGee.

I have nothing against accepting a million-dollar fee and have done so on a number of occasions. But in this case a fee of that size was not justified. (For the record, Kerr-McGee remains our client, and in the eight years since 1982 has paid us handsomely to advise them.)

———

One of the most exciting and challenging jobs was one we failed to get, and it would have involved counseling one of the world's most important and respected figures: the Roman Catholic Pope. What happened was that some very high-ranking Catholic laymen asked me what I thought of the way the Pope's most recent U.S. trip had been handled. As it happened, I didn't think much of it and told them that "It was a disaster."

When they asked why, I gave them a string of reasons. "The Pope has been led to debase himself: There are Pope water sprinklers, and Pope T-shirts, and Pope-on-a-Rope. This is very embarrassing, and doesn't do a thing for religion. It diminishes the position of the Vatican and the Pope in the world."

"Gee," they said, "have you got any suggestions on how to counteract this?" and I said, "Sure. I'd urge the Pope to cut down on his personal appearances, and consider doing a quality television show, using the best of the things that had made Robert Schuller and Pat Robertson so successful. What's more, I'd get good lawyers in every country to go after people who were exploiting the Vatican and get them to stop."

These ideas apparently impressed the Catholic laymen, because they asked me if I would have the nerve to tell the same things to the Pope himself, and I said, of course. As a result, some months later, I found myself ensconced in a marvelous hotel overlooking the Vatican, and while my wife and son had a wonderful time as tourists in Italy, I sat by the phone waiting for the Pope (or his men) to call.

As it turned out, the call never came, for *Il Mondo*, the Italian paper, printed the wholly spurious story that I had been counseling Gorbachev, and that then spelled the end of any possibility of my meeting and counseling the Pope. In my business, like so many others, you don't win them all.

The dictionary defines influence as "power to sway or affect based on prestige, wealth, ability or position." In short, influence means power, the power to make things happen. Advertisers use influence when they try to sell ice cream or toupees. Nancy Reagan uses influence when she urges kids to say no to drugs just as Lech Walesa used influence to score Solidarity's stunning victories in Poland.

Unfortunately, the word *influence* has become synonymous with "influence peddling"—that's unfortunate because influence peddling means the inappropriate use of influence, either influence wrongly used or used for personal gain.

In reality, influence is an indispensable part of everyday life. Used ethically, influence is a formidable skill. Without influence, organizations could not succeed, consensus and coalitions could not be built, and attitudes would never change.

The purpose of this book is twofold. First, it is to explain the realities of influence and how influence works in society and especially in business. Second, it is to give everyone the opportunity to put proven influence tactics to work for themselves.

The use of influence is itself no negative. It can often lead to a great good. Like any powerful force—from potent medicines to nuclear power—it is the morality with which influence is used that makes all the difference.

Often in this book, it will seem as if it was I alone who counseled a world leader or changed the attitude of a major business figure. Many CEOs of major corporations and heads of state only want private counsel, in a one-on-one setting, because the issues are so sensitive. The truth is I am often just "representing" the ideas and views of some very gifted and imaginative thinkers. Indeed, I and Hill and Knowlton's other top managers are supported by a network of hundreds of exceptional professionals worldwide. The lone business counselor is today a rarity and won't be found at Hill and Knowlton. Our business demands top-notch staff work behind it. In fact, John Hill, Hill and Knowlton's founder, cautioned vigorously against falling victim to the ego trip of "The Big I Am"—a worthy precept, and we've adhered to it for decades.

In each of the three very different cases outlined earlier, I, and the people who work with me at Hill and Knowlton, had to decide how best to inform and influence the concerned public.

In the first case, that of the contaminated fruit scare, we had to calm a vast audience of consumers who were worried about a possible threat to their health and that of their children. In the second case, we had to convince a major American corporation "accused" of high crimes that the real target audience it needed to influence with the truth was in fact minuscule. And in the third, we attempted to restore a measure of dignity to one of the essentially most dignified offices in the world, the papacy.

These were very different situations, but each one centered on the use of influence, which is what this book is all about. Before I recount in detail exactly what we did in each of the above situations, I'm going to lay some ground rules. I'm going to introduce you to the principles that are used by public relations professionals in order to solve a major influence crisis or to exert influence in general.

After I have laid that foundation, I'm going to describe how the most successful business managers—in businesses of all sizes—use influence. And then I'll translate that experience into examples and principles that will help *you* advance your own personal business agenda and that of your organization.

In almost all instances, I've tried to reduce the most important principles to rules and axioms based on what I have learned from my own personal experience in twenty-three years in this business, with the last four years spent as chief executive officer of the largest—and, I firmly believe, the best—public relations company in the world.

I will tell you about how I became fascinated by the uses and importance of influence. Talking about myself is not my favorite pastime, but if you are to have faith in the principles I'm about to expound, and if you are to apply them to your own business life, then you need to know how and why I came to believe in them so firmly.

My fascination with influence began at a very early age, as did my direct experience. If you had told me back in the fifties, when I was attending Our Lady of Victory grade school in Columbus, Ohio, that one day I might advise the Pope on the proper use of influence, I would have laughed you out of the schoolyard. (Since the Pope has now personally met with Gorbachev, I think chances are good that I'll be able to present to him personally our fifteen-point program on how he could improve his influence worldwide.)

It's quite possible that my interest in influence in religious circles has its roots in an experience I had in the fifth grade at Our Lady of Victory. I was ten years old, and I used influence to engineer my first "consensus." It was during the season of Lent, the six-week period of fasting and atonement when Catholics prepare for the joyous holiday of Easter Sunday, and the nuns were pressing hard for us to take Holy Communion during mass every day. Those were the days of no meat on Fridays and no food before the day's Communion. Fasting was tough duty, especially for ten-year-olds.

So as soon as mass was over, we would rush downstairs to the "all-purpose room," where the good ladies from the parish sold us a cup of hot chocolate and a donut (for the grand total of 15 cents). Thus revived, we were able to face the day. It seemed a good deal for both sides, as we didn't have to starve until lunchtime, and the ladies made a few dollars.

The nuns, unfortunately, did not see it that way. They decided that our mad dash for such sweet sustenance took too much time and created a disturbance. And if there is one thing that nuns do not like, it is a disturbance. So, led by Sister Mary Euphasia, the nuns lobbied the pastor, Father Favert, and carried the vote. He issued an antidonut dictum: From now on we would go directly to the school from the church, with no sugary side trips. We faced long, hungry hours until lunch.

Clearly, retaliation was in order. With the perfect logic of ten-year-olds, we did the one thing that would most bother the nuns: We stopped going to Communion, or at least enough of us stopped going often enough so that the number of Communions dropped way down. It was a stalemate.

Struck by the seriousness of the situation, I came up with a plan. I organized a group of students that met directly with the pastor and offered my compromise: Instead of racing up and down the stairs, we would buy the hot chocolate and donuts from a hallway table we had to pass on the way back to our rooms. That way, the nuns would get us to Communion, the ladies would get their money, and we would get our beloved donuts!

Father Favert agreed with the plan, and overturned his own donut dictum. I ended up with the reputation of being a good "middle-kid." Throughout high school (St. Charles) and college (Notre Dame) I continued on occasion to display my penchant for being a middle-kid. Today, the term has changed. Now I am called a *facilitator*.

———

The focus of this book will be on how you can learn to exert influence beneficially, in all types of business situations, across the board. But a secondary focus, or subtheme, will be how to do so in crisis situations. I've organized the book to reflect that dual focus for two reasons. One is that in today's business world so many of the problems that can be solved by the adroit use of influence are of the crisis variety. The other reason is that over the past twenty-plus years I have become something of a specialist in crisis solving.

My professional indoctrination into crisis management, and the special joys and sorrows thereof, came very early in my career with Hill and Knowlton. It was the spring of 1969, and rioting had broken out on the campus of Columbia University in New York City.

Dick Darrow, then the head of Hill and Knowlton, had received a call (I don't know if it came on a weekend!) from the head of the Irving Bank, which handled the university's endowment fund. He had received expressions of concern from his own board that the riots would cause businesses and wealthy givers to withdraw their support from Columbia. Could Hill and Knowlton do something about the situation?

Dick Darrow responded by assigning four of us to the job. First, we took the subway (the company has always appreciated expense-account thrift on the part of its employees) to the campus at Morningside Heights for a meeting with Dr. Grayson Kirk, the president of Columbia, and his top aide, David Truman. The two men briefed us on their perception of the problem, which, I soon realized to my surprise, was totally wrong.

They saw the riots as an outgrowth of spring fever. We saw it as just the opposite: the latest in a nationwide eruption of campus riots and violence that was linked, ostensibly at least, to students' feelings about the war in Southeast Asia.

We spent the next several days on campus, talking to anybody and everybody, and as the days passed the disturbances escalated. One morning the police told me that if there was rioting again that evening they planned to sweep the campus and arrest any demonstrators who got in their way.

One more serious night of rioting followed, but then things began to calm down. The subsidence was in large part the result of our activity. We wrote and distributed a long letter that we slipped under the doors of all the students. It told exactly what was happening, and cleared the air of all the rhetoric and cant that had made any sort of meaningful dialogue impossible. I'm convinced that if we had not defused the situation by explaining all the pertinent facts, the students would not have accepted the expulsion of one of their leaders, Mark Rudd, and the rioting would have continued.

The solution to the crisis at Columbia was, for me, an

excellent, if volatile, reaffirmation of the basic lesson that telling the truth is not only the right thing to do but very often it is the smartest thing to do.

———

The Columbia affair taught me another lesson: The media doesn't always play fair. At 1:00 A.M. on the worst night of the rioting, and before we distributed our letter, my immediate Hill and Knowlton boss sent an older colleague and me onto the quadrangle "to get a feel of what's going on."

"Are you crazy?" I said, instinctively. "Can't you see we're in the middle of a full-scale riot?"

"If you don't go out there," he said evenly, "you will no longer have a job at Hill and Knowlton. This is what we expect our people to do."

Bob McCleod, my cohort, was in his early fifties (about twice my age) and not in the best of shape, physically. But we valued our jobs, so out we went. We got to about a hundred yards from the door of the library, our headquarters, when we were spotted by a CBS producer.

The producer signaled a cameraman perched atop the massive Columbia lion in front of the library to turn on his lights. Then, using a bullhorn, he yelled to the students, "See those two guys in the business suits? They're fascist pigs! Get 'em."

Responding on cue, the students began to mass against us. Turning to McCleod, I said, "Let's get these suit jackets off and get back to the library!"

We were about twenty yards from safety when McCleod sank to his knees, one hand grabbing at the front of his shirt. He fell to his knees with what looked very much like a heart attack.

Amidst a shower of tomatoes, eggs, rocks, and bricks, I picked him up and literally carried him the rest of the way to the library. I couldn't resist a shot of sarcasm at my boss. As I dragged Bob McCleod past him, I said, "I think I know what's happening out there."

In spite of this incident, I very much enjoy working with the media. Much of my time is spent working closely with print journalists or radio and television people, and I have great respect for the majority of them. In fact, I almost became a journalist myself. My father was a journalist who passed his love for the profession down to me.

I learned the importance of dealing with the press, and its fundamental relationship to influence, at an early age. My dad started with the *Rockville Leader*, in Rockville, Connecticut, and then moved to Philadelphia where he worked for the *Ledger* and the *Inquirer*, and then to New York City, where I was born, to work for Scripps Howard.

During my earliest years, we lived first in Kew Gardens, New York, and then we moved to Forest Hills, which is quite well known as the former site of the U.S. Open in tennis. In Forest Hills, we lived on the same street as Vic Lombardo, Guy's brother and a member of his band. As a matter of fact, Mr. Lombardo lived on one side of us and on the other lived a man named Mike Johnson. Mike wrote a Pulitzer Prize–winning series in 1949 which became the basis for the movie *On the Waterfront*. Years later, his son Haynes also won a Pulitzer in the reporting category. As my father was fond of bringing interesting, literate people to the house for dinner, I grew up in an atmosphere surrounded by newspapers and books and literary talk.

In 1948, when I was about four or five, Scripps Howard transferred my dad to Cleveland to run the *Cleveland Press* with the legendary editor Louis Seltzer. In 1950, the family moved from Cleveland to Columbus, where my father ran the *Columbus Citizen*, and my interest in journalism grew, in large part because the town was filled with competing newspapers. Ohio State football was a major item of interest, and the *Citizen* fought the *Ohio State Journal* and the *Columbus Dispatch* for readers. It was a rocking town, with newsboys on the streets hawking papers at 8:00 at night. I loved it.

Columbus, Ohio, became my adopted home town. It was there that I attended both grade school and high school. It was there that I first became aware of how far-reaching was the question of influence. It wasn't just the press, or politics, or business that intrigued me. It was something broader: how views were presented and how they were reconciled. Thus, for as long as I can remember, I have been studying the role of influence in solving problems.

That study has taken me down some very interesting roads. In the twenty-three years I've been with Hill and Knowlton—first in New York, then in Chicago for seven very special years, and now back in New York as the company's chief executive officer—I've worked with such diverse groups as the AFL-CIO, the Securities and Exchange Commission, the Federal Reserve Board, IBM, the U.S. Supreme Court, Jesse Jackson's Rainbow Coalition, the Vatican, and the Politburo. I have turned down requests for help from the Mob, the Ton-Ton Macoutes, and General Noriega.

Thus, I have learned some very simple truths. One is that the key to having influence is to get people to focus on a problem that is clearly and simply stated (and usually you are the one who has done the clarifying and the stating). Then you find out why the issue is so emotionally important to the people involved; and, finally, you offer a solution that satisfies all the parties needed to make the solution work.

Along with learning all the little tricks that go into effectuating that simple-sounding formula, I also managed to pick up a love for my company and my profession. When I see a public relations firm representing General Noriega, despite the CIA's documentation that he is contributing to the drug problem in the United States, I cringe. When I see a public relations firm working for some company they know is Mob-owned, I cringe. When I see Mike Milken inviting paraplegic kids out to Yankee Stadium in what appears to me to be a device to change his image, I cringe. I am deeply troubled because I know how such representations make the public feel about the profession I love.

I have an unalterable faith in the honor of my profession. Last August I wrote a short letter to all my managers that I would like to share with you.

Dear _____ :

I want to talk to you about something important—ethics.

Most of us think of ethics as the practical application of the moral principles we believe in. For example, we treat others as we want to be treated ourselves as a matter of principle rather than as a requirement of society. It is a sound approach to relationships, whether on a personal, professional, or business level.

As our institutions mature and grow more demanding of acceptable human behavior, some ethical principles are becoming imposed on society as requirements rather than simply good form or personal attributes expected of educated men and women.

A recent example is the voluntary agreement by a major U.S. corporation to publicly apologize to an individual and pay handsomely after planting false stories about him. This was evidently done to avoid a trial on the issue in a court of law. Another example is of a $100 million fine imposed by a jury on still another major company that falsely claimed a vendor had deliberately harmed it. These two examples are part of a growing litany of similar instances. And regardless of who was responsible for these acts, these cases tell us that mudslinging on the business scene is no longer simply unethical; it can be a costly and illegal activity.

This is a message most Hill and Knowlton people will note with only passing interest because we have always maintained that a high ethical standard of conduct is a first principle of good public relations. Yet there may be occasions when account executives and managers are under pressure from less fastidious clients to knock the competition. The temptation to waver can be strong because of the fear of losing profitable business, and perhaps even because the client's competitor plays a dirty game.

Moreover, we are all tempted from time to time to remark unfavorably about the activities, claims, or tactics of competitors in our own field, which can sometimes be annoying, underhanded, misleading or even unethical. The natural reaction to such conduct is to refute it, if possible, or deplore it when asked for comment. No matter what the facts are, however, whatever is said by Hill and Knowlton about a competitor will always appear to be the bully-boy picking on the little guy.

So, as a matter of good business—as well as acceptable ethics—we must always be circumspect when commenting about the competition, whether it be a client's competitor or one of our own. This is not to say we must praise the unpraiseworthy, nor must we find the bright side of a dark act brought against us or a client. On the other hand, there is never an acceptable excuse for deliberately traducing the competition or going along with the criticism of others.

The only conduct we can control is our own, and it is imperative that it be—and be seen to be—always in the high end of the ethical scale. *And it is our responsibility to urge the same conduct on our clients.*

Because you are the leaders of this Firm, and you are controlling recommendations to clients, I expect that you will see to it that Hill and Knowlton *never* recommends to clients conduct that is less than totally acceptable, both ethically and legally.

I expect you to share this thinking with your staff.

When Hill and Knowlton was a tiny Firm back in the 1940s, and its owners desperate to expand the business, founder John W. Hill wrote: "It is my firm conviction that under no foreseeable circumstances will the demands for good public relations services diminish. I stress the word *good* because that is going to be the criterion of the future. My idea of *good* is being effective, combined with high standards of ethics and sound judgment."

He was prophetic and, in my opinion, largely because the Firm he founded has never varied from his definition of what is good in public relations, not the least of which is maintaining a high standard of ethics.

Best regards,

Robert L. Dilenschneider

Part I

RECOGNIZING THE INFLUENTIAL MANAGER

1

The Power Triangle

General Motors Chairman Roger Smith, in order to revamp a massive company, has invested huge amounts in automation and undertaken enormous reorganizations. Smith's programs have not won enthusiastic approval, and GM's communications shortcomings have often been cited in the press. Smith himself has candidly conceded the weakness in print, stating that if he had the chance to repeat his major restructuring of GM he would do exactly the same thing. But, he says in a *Fortune* article, "I sure wish I'd done a better job of communicating with GM people. I'd do that differently a second time around and make sure they understood my vision for the company. . . . There we were charging up the hill right on schedule, and I looked behind me and saw that many people were still at the bottom, trying to decide whether to come along."

In 1982, International Harvester—the farm equipment manufacturer now known as Navistar—faced very tough times. They were reeling from international competition and slackening sales in their core business lines. Archie McCardell, Harvester's CEO, responded with aggressive expense cutting.

3

He went against the union and demanded wage rollbacks. Undoubtedly, McCardell worked very hard, and he deserved to be rewarded at some point, but the question was: When? Lynn O'Shea, Harvester's communications head at the time, asked me what I thought about a plan to give Archie McCardell a bonus of one million dollars. I pointed out that in light of the fact that union workers were chipping in pennies per hour to keep the business afloat, giving such a huge bonus would send a very negative signal about McCardell and Harvester. I warned them that if they gave the bonus it would haunt them. Not long after that, McCardell was ousted.

Since that time Navistar's CEOs Don Lennox and Jim Cotting, with shrewd assistance from their public relations chiefs Annette De Lorenzo and Mary Moster, have brought this fine company back. But the legacy of Archie's mistake haunts the halls as a reminder of how not to do it.

Former U.S. Senator John Tower had been nominated for Secretary of Defense. At a televised hearing, he put his hand on the knee of a woman who was not his wife. At one point, both his former wife and another female acquaintance were seen sitting behind him at the confirmation hearings. He offered to cut a deal: He pledged to stop drinking if confirmed as Secretary of Defense. Tower's actions and his statements failed to communicate to the public and the Senate that he had the right character for the Defense post.

Asbestos, the ubiquitous flame-retardant material, was linked with cancer and other dangerous diseases. Johns Manville, its largest producer, became the target of countless lawsuits. Rather than take an aggressive position, explain the problem, and state

4

what was being done to correct it—as Johnson & Johnson did when it was hit by the Tylenol crisis—Manville management headed for the bunker. Communication was stonewalled. Manville was tried in the press and sentenced to Chapter Eleven. As George Melloan reported in the *Wall Street Journal*, in the end, it will give up $2.5 billion, 20 percent of its future profits, and 80 percent of its stock.

In order to influence opinion, you have to be an able communicator. If you can't communicate, you won't influence opinion. And if you can't influence opinion, you won't get very far in management.

What do people who are able to exert influence and advance their careers know? What is the secret that they understand so well? I would say that they grasp a very simple relationship: the connection between communication, recognition, and influence. I describe that relationship as *the power triangle*.

To be a good communicator, you don't have to be a great orator. One CEO I counsel suffers from such stage fright that he won't ask for money for the United Way unless he does it on videotape. Still, he's a good communicator. He uses his influence effectively and controls the agenda of his business. He knows what matters to people and how to resolve problems.

Some people would say this CEO only knows how to manage, but I've been a CEO watcher for some time, and I know that the secret of his success is more basic than that. He knows how to *communicate*, and that's why he manages so well. Communication is the more fundamental skill.

Many managers believe communication is how you say it. But communication is not style, not the elegance of your letterhead any more than the eloquence of your speech. Rather, communication is the very heart of management. It is solid thinking translated into clear messages.

Sloppy thinking and weak strategy—not poor style—cause the biggest communications mistakes. I began this chapter with a list of some of the worst boners in management communications in recent years. And they have nothing to do with dangling participles, limp body language, or the color of the shirt worn on television. In each of these cases, communications boners had a material impact on the future of a business or a career, and sometimes both.

Communications *triumphs* can help make careers, and I'll also tell you about triumphs. So often, influence and success depend on making communications a deliberate act, which means anticipating what reporters or any other audience will do with what you say or how you behave.

Much can be learned about the importance of influence and communications from executive recruiters. I work closely with recruiters who do top management placements. They know that every step closer to the top demands a new and higher level of skill in influence and communications. In fact, at the very top it is the *central* management skill.

J. Curtis Fee, a senior director in the Chicago office of Spencer Stuart, believes that the capacity to exert influence is absolutely necessary to function as a CEO; it's as taken for granted as a college degree. It's also essential to progressing to each successive level up the management ladder. Conducting a search for a top manager includes weighing many factors, technical and managerial. But, an overriding consideration in Fee's mind is "the ability to be taken seriously." He believes that this is an innate part of a person's makeup and is tantamount to exerting influence. "It comes out when you're in the sixth grade and the kids are choosing up sides for a softball game." After observing a meeting, a skilled recruiter should be able to pinpoint those who have the ability to influence from those who don't "as clearly as if the participants were wearing signs around their necks," Curt contends.

Bill Bowen, who is vice-chairman of Heidrick & Struggles, has told me, "There are certain influence patterns that I think are common to all good top managers. First, they must have strong self-esteem. To lead, a top manager needs a strong ego, but that manager must also know how to reign it in. I listen carefully to the verbal cues of this ego balance. If a manager describes the achievements of his company as 'we tackled this tough technology problem,' or if he explains accomplishment as 'I ... I ... I.'" To me that boils down to skill in getting recognition—an essential factor in having influence.

"Communications has clearly become the number one aptitude of the CEO, and this is true for several reasons," Bill adds. "First, CEOs become CEOs earlier than they used to, and the same is true of other top managers. When Walter Wriston left Citicorp, people were amazed at the relative youth of the top management team compared with what they had been used to. People nicknamed Citicorp 'Kiddycorp,' but what happened at Citicorp and other forward-looking institutions rapidly became the trend in industry. Second, more and more CEOs particularly did not grow up in the companies that they are running. They have moved around a bit—often to three or four different firms. Third, they can burn out faster—they are more vulnerable than they used to be." More mobile and younger CEOs must rely more heavily on communications to exert influence. What goes for CEOs also holds to an equally important extent for all managers. Our predecessors leaned more on seniority, familiarity with the firm's culture, and technical skills. Today's top manager is often "shallow" in each of these suits.

American business is hungry for leaders comfortable with exerting influence at an early age. These sought-after managers know how to symbolize leadership and project characteristics that companies admire. Look at *Fortune*'s "On the Rise" column. These are men and women who know how to embody the values their companies want and need, which is an integral part of career strategy. The more effective a person is in symbolizing leadership and influence, the higher he* is likely to rise in his organization.

The first step to influence is communication. Communication is very broadly defined, but it is, in this case, a study about yourself or your company. When you give a speech, you are communicating. When you perform a favor, you are also communicating. When you visit with the rank-and-file workers in your department, you are communicating, sending a signal. When you attack your competitor as a villain, you are also communicating. If you are communicating effectively, you will get positive recognition for your communication from the audiences you are trying to influence, which means people will think what you are doing is right and that you are doing it in the right way. When you get positive recognition, your influence grows. You are perceived as competent, effective, worthy of respect—*powerful.* Power comes from remembering and using the linkage of communication, recognition, and influence.

If you want to extend your influence you must do two things. First, you have to keep your overall level of communication up to your highest standards. Second, you must focus your communication. The more focused your communication is, the deeper the impression it will make. The deeper the impression, the better the odds are that you will be recognized.

To achieve focus, you must have a plan. I call that plan an agenda. Unlike the typical plan, you never really complete a particular point on an agenda. You don't check it off a list. Let's say that you want to make "being a community leader" a focal point on your agenda. If you are successful, your

---

*For ease of reading, in general I will use the masculine form of the pronoun although I am, obviously, referring to both sexes.

community leadership role never goes away. Instead, it gets bigger, more powerful, and more selective. Over time, the focal points of your agenda will shift. Both company and personal agendas will rarely have more than four or five points. The art of influence is defining, realizing, and gradually strengthening your personal agenda.

2

The Favor Bank

I am indebted to Tom Wolfe for this term. He coined it in his novel *The Bonfire of the Vanities*. As the old saw goes, "What goes around comes around." As Tom Wolfe explains the Favor Bank, it "means if you don't take care a me today, I won't take care a you tomorrow." It captures an essential element in how the world of influence works. And, it means simply that you had better be able to deliver favors—to draw on the Favor Bank—if you want to have influence. As Bert Lance, who headed the office of the budget for the Carter White House, explained to me once, "You have to expend capital for what you need to do." That capital, of course, can be of many sorts, but often it is using influence to solve a problem.

Bert Lance understands the Favor Bank very well. In fact, I suspect that he is a reigning trustee of the Bank. Walk down any street in the South with Bert—in Charlotte, Mobile, or wherever—and local leaders, from high-tech CEOs to car-wash managers, will walk up and say an enthusiastic hello. Past the door of his relatively modest Calhoun, Georgia, home you will find an entryway to a huge study.

The floor is covered with the famous Oval Office rug that bears the presidential seal with its sprawling eagle. Inside the office are a network of personal computers and telephones that would put the National Security Council to shame. The man knows the routes to power. He's on the phone all day—to Canberra, Tel Aviv, and Rijadh. He can trade in the Favor Bank with the same ease that a Morgan Stanley can make markets in foreign currency.

Bert and others have taught me a great deal about how the Favor Bank works and the rules that go along with it. Here are some of the most important ones I've learned.

Be responsive, not offensive. Membership in the "club" is hard to come by; so is hanging on to the keys. As Bert says, "There's a waiting list out there and a lot of talent trying to find their way on to it." Be responsive. Though it might not be today, some day you might need the president of the Louisville Red Cross to go to bat for you. Every time you offend someone, you create a potential foe who may one day block your admission into the "club," that circle of influential people at any given level.

Support the "rainmakers." When Rabbi Arthur Schneier (one of the most influential men in New York and president of the Appeal of Conscience Foundation) called me on a Sunday afternoon and asked if Hill and Knowlton would help lead the Armenian relief effort (after the devastating 1988 earthquake), it took me one second to say yes. The same thing happened when IBM's retired CEO Frank Cary asked for our help on a project in New York City. First, it was right to take on both projects. Second, it has paid off handsomely in how we are regarded. Third, it was answering a rainmaker's call. If you want to maintain an active balance at the Favor Bank, jump when a rainmaker calls.

Figure out whom you need and who needs you. There are two kinds of balances you can draw on in the Favor Bank. Consider the first to be your personal account—the balance you build up by doing favors for others. The second is your corporate account, which is the balance you get for your company simply by being in your position. If you're the CEO, or even a middle manager, there are plenty of people who need you and your company's business. Surprisingly, most people underestimate who needs them. Just think about it. In any business situation, there are a remarkable number of vendors and suppliers who make their living because of your business. Of course, I'm not suggesting you lean on these people for bribes or theater tickets. But, you should leverage these resources for aboveboard advantages and favors that can advance your business.

Draw on the Favor Bank to ease change. Every time you face an important change, are launching a program, or must confront a big problem, you should create an agenda for change. Next to each point on the agenda, you should mark down which of the people who need you can help make that change or resolution easier, more effective, and/or less expensive.

People will do plenty for you. Most will do it without a fee, if you make two things clear: You don't intend to pay a fee for the service and you really appreciate what they are doing. Maybe you are based in Cleveland, and you want to add a plant in Romania. You need intelligence on the tax codes in that country. Let's say your auditor is a Big Six accounting firm. Any Big Six firm would turn somersaults to help you anywhere in their vast global network just to defend their audit fee. There will certainly come a point when the firm will tell you that you have overextended your welcome, but have you even approached that point today?

Are you concerned that a public policy issue may become a grave threat to your company? Have you asked the think tank that you're funding in your contributions program for their analysis of the problem? Maybe a neighborhood community leader has become a very visible opponent of your affirmative action plans. Is she the same civic leader who also chairs the community outreach program of the symphony orchestra to which you contribute so generously? Look at the minefield of threats to your business and then look at who's already out there taking the king's shilling. Chances are that you're now funding or retaining the organization or individual who can take care of your problem. If you ask the right way, these are people who can help you with customers, the government, regulators, perhaps even the press.

Tap the Favor Bank only with authorization. No manager should impose on his company's Favor Bank account before checking with the CEO or a top officer. It's at that level that the Favor Bank balances are kept. The brass may think you have a great idea, but not checking it out first could cost you your career.

Look for favors you can do. Continually pay attention to both sides of the Favor Bank ledger. Constantly look for favors that you can perform for others that don't cost you anything. Who are the powerful people who feel really antagonistic toward your business? I'm talking about special-interest leaders, columnists, politicians—anyone who can be a big-league aggravation. Without undermining your business objectives, do every possible favor you can for these people. It's done every day by top managers in the Fortune 500.

Maintain a good "credit rating." I get my share of calls from Favor Bank deadbeats who ask for many more favors than they should. Trade association heads are notorious for this! If you're an active trader in the Bank, it's not easy to stay in the black. How do you keep on top? Look for ways to maneuver the good with the bad. Sometimes I need a powerful institution like the Council on Foreign Relations to do me a favor. The finance minister from a Scandinavian country may want to speak at a prestigious U.S. forum, but his message is most routine. Simply put, I need someone to help eat a loss. Usually, I can get the job done. How? I will feed the organization something very good in advance. A top economist calls me up and says he's ready with a new slant on the economy. I contact a trend-setting publication and promise him for an exclusive interview. I'll also go out of my way to secure another, hotly sought-after speaker for the council to make up for the ho-hum one. Leading publications and organizations such as the council understand the unwritten rule. That's how you keep up your credit rating so it can withstand the occasional hits.

Deposit "intellectual capital" on the way up. Senior executives get a lot of mileage in their community through leveraging their company's contributions program. Some companies have matching grants for all their employees that let everyone share in the company's contribution influence. But, what if you're just a young manager with no wad of money to give away? Are there ways to build up your personal account in the Favor Bank? Indeed, there are. It's called trading in "intellectual capital."

Let's say you are a rising executive, and you want to make your impact felt on a politician. You know that you can't make a heavyweight financial contribution. But, can you help him in designing his fund-raising strategy? Can you spend your evening hours researching a particular topic so he can write a blockbuster speech?

Your community hospital can't afford a financial analysis function, but you hear that the trustees (who are also the most powerful community leaders) blame serious operating problems on lack of good analysis. Can you step in and offer your expertise to troubleshoot the problem?

Has your most important customer long wanted to restore the pipe organ in the landmark theater down the street? Can you compensate for his lack of skill in organizing community projects by putting together a workable plan to raise the money?

For managers at every level, there is a way to leverage intelligence and ingenuity for impact far beyond your apparent "rank." Sweat-equity staff work is often the way to tone up the influence of a manager on the come.

Get credit for your favors. I am called to assess a candidate for a senior management job at a major bank. I give him a strong recommendation, and they say he's at the top of the short list. I immediately call the candidate and tell him he's likely to get the job. Who do you think the candidate will think helped him cinch the position?

Deposit regularly and heavily in the Favor Bank. We all know that business is getting more complicated, which ensures that we will all be caught in more jams in the most unexpected places—with fire marshals, phone companies, EPA officials, and regional media. Make an inventory of your coming "rainy days," and then figure out whom you should be inviting to lunch.

Advertise your Favor Bank balance. It's not enough to have a balance in the Favor Bank; it pays to advertise it. In a speech, you will hear an executive say, "When the local high school needed hardware for its PC curriculum, we were glad to donate it. It was nothing less than an investment in the community." At a board meeting, a director will comment, "We gave this particular cabinet secretary a real assist in rallying our industry around his position. I'd be happy to see if he can help dig you out of this regulatory scrape." Both of these are soft-sell advertisements for power and influence. Influential people are always touting that important organizations and people owe them favors, which amplifies their influence even more. Of course, this must be done discreetly and with caution not to oversell. And most of all, it has to be true!

Always build goodwill. Many people abuse their Favor Bank balance by being hotheads. Before you send off a searing complaint to a network, a magazine, or even another firm in your community, have a communications specialist look at it to make sure it furthers your own company's interest. How will the letter look in print or sound on the air? More than one executive has written a poison-pen complaint to some CEO, only to have that same letter boomerang back to his own CEO with a none-too-happy note about the bad-mouther. At the very least, check to make sure that the CEO of the firm you're attacking doesn't sit on your own company's board. Anger can be costly. Remember at least the first part of the Kennedy golden rule, "Don't get mad, get even."

Build balances abroad. The Favor Bank has gone global and your Favor credit card better be welcome abroad. Following the trend of business itself, it's very important for managers to establish contacts abroad, and it will be even more so in future years. If you are a middle-level or even junior manager, cultivate foreign contacts at symposiums or conferences. The United States is still the world center for management education. Any alert manager will find the opportunity to make a large number of foreign contacts right here in the States. Even if you are linked with relatively junior people from Austria or India, you can bet they will die trying to connect you with the most important people they can—as a show of their own influence.

Imagine yourself at a management meeting inside your own company. You are a lower-level analyst. Expansion plans in Australia come up. Your company is in the building trades, and management wants to know how to interpret data they have on home loans in Sydney. Your eyes light up, and you say that you met an Australian bank analyst at a recent American Management Association conference. You have a good relationship, and you know he'll help you get some data. Will your management see you as a person who knows how to make the contacts that lead to influence? You bet they will!

In many foreign cultures, especially in the Far East and Mediterranean Europe, favors are an even more important part of the fabric of business than in the United States. Who you know really shows your influence, so if such a country is in your career game plan, start building your contacts early.

3

Tough Managers and Temperamental Managers

I was once summoned to Pittsburgh with several of my colleagues. Our task was to advise a CEO on how to deal with a labor relations crisis. The CEO was a mean-spirited man, given to venomous tirades, and I was not unhappy that a sixteen-foot oak conference table separated us, as I was to propose the most controversial recommendation. That recommendation was to recognize that many of the union's demands were legitimate. Management was oblivious to what was happening on the shop floor. We proposed that the company own up to its own shortcomings in a responsible but firm way. I wanted the company to set a timetable for acting on specific union proposals. I also said that the CEO would probably continue to have serious trouble unless he got his top lieutenants out to the bullpens regularly.

He didn't like what we recommended. And, I think that he found the distance between the two of us especially frustrating. Without warning, halfway through the presentation, he hurled a three-pound lead crystal ashtray at me. Badly thrown, it sailed by

19

my head, missing me by at least two feet, but it succeeded in shattering a floor-to-ceiling pane of glass, spraying shards of window on the shrubbery outside the meeting room like icicles on a Christmas tree.

I was stunned. I didn't know how to respond. But, I suddenly heard myself saying, "Do you mind if I close the drapes? I don't want it to be too drafty for you while we finish our presentation." My seeming composure must have shocked the client. He sank back in his chair, listened to the rest of the presentation without a word, and bought the program about twenty minutes later. Sometimes it pays just to ignore outrage, especially when you don't know what to do about it.

I have worked for one tough bunch of managers. About ten years ago, *Fortune* published its first list of the ten toughest bosses in America. *Fortune* has published three separate "short lists" of the toughest CEOs. Twenty-seven company heads appear on those three lists. I have counseled eleven of those toughest twenty-seven managers—such people as Bob Abboud, who today is president of First Bancorporation of Texas; Bob Crandall at AMR (American Airlines); and Dick Mahoney at Monsanto. It may not surprise you that most of the tough managers with whom I've worked are successful. It might surprise you that they are all good communicators. They have had the guts to come out and talk straight to their employees. On the other hand, I have had a few clients who played at being tough, but were just impulsive and temperamental, like my ashtray hurler. The influential manager knows how to be tough, but tough in a constructive way.

Have a tough hide. That means being able to conceal your feelings when the situation calls for it. The higher up you go,

the more the people around you will tell you what you want to hear. You will be lucky to have one advisor who tells you the truth. The truth will hurt.

People won't truly understand the actions you take. They will interpret your move in their own ways. I will never forget the reaction of Jim Paasch, a Weyerhaeuser plant manager in Kalamazoo, Michigan. Paasch had been ordered to shut down the plant in an orderly way. In the process, the employees painted Paasch as an evil ogre. He was doing his job and doing it well. But, when his friends told him what people thought of him and his actions, he actually tried to block the closing of the plant. Weyerhaeuser is a wonderful company, but I'm sure it questioned Paasch's judgment. You can't afford to let being unpopular get to you.

Treat controversy with respect. There is no point in getting embroiled in controversy unless there is a clear gain to be had from it. The Japanese are setting the management style of the 1990s, and the watchword of Japanese management is *harmony*. Companies want leaders with backbone, but they also want managers who can achieve and sustain a harmonious workplace.

Don't let the bully face you down. And, remember, the bully can be a subordinate as often as a superior or a peer. I have seen many a manager cowed by an opportunistic subordinate, thus losing status and influence. About a year ago, an executive in our firm wrote me a letter. I got it just before Thanksgiving. In the letter, he listed eight demands. They were outrageous demands: everything from his joining the board of the company to a tripling of his salary. He concluded his letter with a flourish: "If my issues are not resolved by December 15, I will be leaving the company." I didn't answer the letter. On December 15, he stopped by to see me. After he came in and sat down, he waited for me to start the conversation. I just sat there. After about a minute, he cleared his throat and asked, "Have you read my letter?" I said yes. "Well?" he pressed ahead. I then said, "I assume you are leaving. I've taken you off the payroll. You have no role in the future of our organization. I simply can't do what you told me had to happen. You've done a helluva job, but you have made it impossible for me to meet your needs. You told me you had to leave, so I resigned myself to it two weeks ago." The guy is still with our firm . . . but he is a little chastened.

Sometimes, bullying can take unaccustomed shapes. The snub is a form of bullying, and I go out of my way to reject a snub. I think it's wrong not to stand up for your own dignity. When someone attempts to snub me in public—and people have—I try to find some clever way to parry with them. I'll even do the same in private, when no one is watching. I remember being alone in a room with a very patrician Canadian banker once. We were both presenters on the same conference agenda, waiting for our respective turns to speak with absolutely nothing to do. I tried breaking the silence with a question about the trade bill the Canadian parliament was debating. He handed back a contemptuous "hrrmph" and turned away. A couple of minutes passed, and I tried another gambit about the importance of Canadian hydroelectric power. Five minutes more of stony silence. Then, I took a pad of paper, wrote a short note on it, and handed it to him. In an instant, his face turned red with rage . . . and just as quickly, he exploded in laughter and broke into conversation about the Expos. He decided he had no choice but to be civil. On the slip of paper I had written, "I can do this just as long as you can."

There are serious results of a snub, too. Three months before the Grand Met takeover of Pillsbury, I tried to call the Doughboy's CEO, Phil Smith, to let him know precisely what was going to happen. We had learned Grand Met's exact plans, and at that point Grand Met was not yet a client of ours. Smith wouldn't take my call. So, I went to a Pillsbury outside director I knew. But, the outside director, a would-be purist who had an aversion for public relations, refused to alert Smith that he knew my name. That snub helped cost Smith his company, and certainly cost his shareholders several points on their stock. Five months after the deal was done, I passed a message to the outside director about what his inaction had cost Pillsbury management. He pleaded with me to keep his identity quiet. So far, I have.

Pick your fights. Whom you fight with determines your stature. Your opponents tell the world who you are. During the Disney takeover attempt, a lawyer, Stanley P. Gold, got into a dispute with William F. Buckley, Jr. As noted in John Taylor's *Storming the Magic Kingdom*, [Buckley], who was far better known than Gold, "told a reporter for the *Wall Street Journal* that Gold was 'full of crap.' Gold clipped the article and hung it on his study wall. 'Anybody who's called full of crap in the *Wall Street Journal*, by no less a person than William Buckley, has arrived,' his wife, Ilene, told him."

Practice! As with every aspect of management, there is no substitute for experience, but there are ways to prepare your mind. When you watch the evening news or read a publication, think about how a leader or a spokesperson handled a belligerent question or explained an embarrassing problem:

> Would you have handled it the same way?

> Would you have given out the same amount of information? Less? More?

> Would you have tried to answer the question or said you simply didn't know?

> How could you have simplified the explanation?

You can learn a great deal from this kind of second-guessing . . . and these lessons are, after all, free.

4

Image Quacks

In the spring of 1989, *Harper's* featured an irreverent spoof on how Christ's second coming might be "image packaged." The first suggestion "is that he come back an older man—rounder of figure (cuddlier), some gray hair (wiser) and shorter hair (modern)." His first tour outfit should have a "woven gold collar to reinforce the idea of the halo" and he should wear "generic tennis shoes to show humor, energy, comfort, individuality, and youth." His "casual look" outfit is built around a "natural wool fisherman's knit sweater." Adelle Lutz's parody points out just how much nonsense is wrapped up in image counseling.

I have long opposed any kind of advisor who works on a manager's image separate from that manager's "content." But image consulting has become a growth industry of massive proportions. As reported in the *New York Times*, *Image Industry Publications*, the trade journal that follows this business, estimates that there are three hundred companies, billing $130 million a year in revenues, who do such things as analyze wardrobe color, rethink your jewelry, and reconstruct your "total visual presentation"—from your Oxford suits to your Mont Blanc fountain pens.

I suspect this obsession with appearance as the road to influence took off with John T. Molloy's book, *Dress for Success*, back in 1977, though Theodore White's books on the making of presidents explore how appearance affects power before Molloy's book. No doubt, personal appearance has a bearing on a manager's influence potential, but sensibility and traditional good grooming are, I think, far more likely to achieve success than any image makeover scheme.

The image industry contends that about a million people a year use the services of the so-called image consultants. Actors, cosmeticians, benched athletes, and cultists pepper the ranks of the image doctors. For fees of hundreds and sometimes thousands of dollars, these "experts" will review your wardrobe and teach you "power gestures" such as the JFK curlicue or the golf grip handshake. A *Washington Post* article describes these wrinkles as "mannerisms designed to rivet the attention of one person or an audience of hundreds." The image pundits will tell you if your hairdo is too soft or your speech is too brash. Image expert Camille Lavington offers this advice in the *New York Times*: "Let people see your face. Men should get rid of beards and sideburns; women should get rid of bangs. Your power center in business is your head."

I have long believed that your "power center in business" is indeed your head, except it is what's in your head, not what's on or around it, that matters.

Understand how people see things, then appeal to what they prefer. The key to real image strategy is understanding the link between how people see and what people prefer. Here's a very simple example. People prefer to associate with honest people over dishonest people. They have also been trained to suspect, that is to "see," that a man with a black shirt, a heavy gold neck chain, dark glasses, and a bulge under the jacket is a mobster. Many people would avoid a man dressed that way because he fits an undesirable stereotype. Packard Vance provides a more subtle example: People prefer to think of themselves as more durable than the everyday goods they use. A major luggage maker some years ago wanted to stress the durability of its bags. The firm dramatized this by dropping a piece of luggage out of a flying airplane. The bag bounced harmlessly and came through in great shape, but consumers were unnerved by the ad. What they "saw" was their luggage surviving an airplane accident that they personally never could. The bag was projecting an improper image of strength.

People can project improper images just as products can. When he took his million-dollar bonus, Archie McCardell was projecting greed instead of compassion and sacrifice. John Tower exhibited willfulness more than judgment. These people didn't pay attention to what people saw and preferred, and they lost. The color of their ties and the firmness of their handshakes had nothing to do with their fates.

Approach dress and etiquette sensibly. A sturdy guidebook on dress and etiquette that I have long recommended to businesspeople was penned by Letitia Baldridge, who was once Jacqueline Kennedy's chief of staff. The book is called *Letitia Baldridge's Complete Guide to Executive Manners* (Rawson Associates, 1985), and it will tell you what to do when a Japanese manager dies, how to dress for the swimming pool at a management retreat, and why you should never touch an Arab sheik with your left hand. There are times you need to know these things, and it's useful to be able to look them up. But a lot of unnecessary and expensive nonsense on image building has been fabricated. An obsession with it can actually derail an executive from the serious issues of influence.

Use setting to support image. Beyond sensible etiquette, the "cosmetics" add little to influence. In contrast, the cosmetics of the environment around you can make a great difference. Sometimes you want that setting to be opulent. When Japanese car makers Nissan and Toyota decided to enter the luxury car market, dealers developed new, more glamorous showrooms to highlight their new luxury image. *Forbes* reported that Nissan mandated use of granite for some of the display area at $17 a foot, which was a shrewd decision.

A great deal of money and thinking went into designing Ronald Reagan's speaking podium to make it look powerful but also soft and understated (no sharp corners, for example). But the plushest setting is not necessarily the best. I recall a huge chemical fire that had gutted an impoverished, backwater town in the South. The network coverage flipped from the nightmarish scene of screaming children and scorched shacks back to the company's headquarters. There the CEO stood answering questions in front of the company's gleaming marble office building with its dreamy landscape of manicured trees and bushes. He had been set up by a shrewd news crew who wanted to exploit the contrast. Later that morning, I called the CEO, who was not a client, and pointed out what had been done to him. It was as if a brick hit him in the forehead. From that point forward, all interviews with company spokespersons, including the CEO, were done at the disaster site.

Study the masters of image "downscaling." I never condone trying to manipulate your image upward. I generally recommend not trying to manipulate your personal image at all. But I still must acknowledge that some very shrewd people have been able to manipulate their image to their advantage by "downscaling" it—making it less imposing or threatening.

Some of the best image manipulators are ones you would never suspect. Georgia O'Keeffe affords an outstanding example. Edward Abrahams wrote of O'Keeffe in the *New*

Republic that she "had controlled almost every element of her public image, and of our understanding of her place in the history of American art. . . . According to the myth she helped create, O'Keeffe cared little for society or material wealth, never compromised her integrity, owed nothing to anyone." Abrahams writes that O'Keeffe very carefully selected the agents who represented her, controlled the biographical treatments written about her, censored where her art was to appear, and managed her relations with the media very effectively.

Do I condone O'Keeffe's apparent methods? Well, I have several reactions to them. First, I admire her skill in creating such a successful image while she was alive, but her story also shows that the most ingenious image campaigns will be found out sooner or later. If the image she created was a false one, you certainly can't admire that. But, even if it was false, it can take nothing away from her superior achievements as an artist. (Whenever I think of duplicity and the arts, I remember that even such a lofty spirit as Beethoven has been accused of trying to sell the same work to two publishers.)

Don't be *too* smart. Jean de la Bruyere once said, "A man has made great progress in cunning, when he does not seem too clever to others." T. Boone Pickens and Orville Redenbacher know how to leverage the homespun. CEOs who have a need to lecture or to display their vast technical knowledge are tough acts in front of an audience. They build up a wall between themselves and the people they are trying to reach. The public readily accepts an intellectual such as Henry Kissinger or Zbigniew Brzezinski in a secondary or staff role, but wouldn't tolerate a polished intellectual as CEO of the country.

Project a consistent image. Forget the phony, juiced-up power image. Concentrate instead on projecting a consistent image. Unpredictable people undermine their own influence. When

Frank Borman was CEO of Eastern Airlines, he laid heavy emphasis on customer service and "earning our wings every day." Yet, when Borman spoke to his own employees at meetings, he frequently used coarse language, peppered with obscenities. His message and his style were inconsistent. Other leaders derive great strength from their consistency. Among them are Mikhail Gorbachev, John Johnson (publisher of *Ebony*), Ford CEO "Red" Poling, and Simon Murray (CEO of Hutchison). They present a continuous style in everything they do and in all the places they are heard: books, public appearances, personal conversations, press releases, and all the other channels.

5

Influence
and Integrity

Ivan Boesky called us when he was headed for jail.
He wanted to see if PR could help cushion the skids.
We told him that there were a number of other
great agencies in New York and he should use them.

A well-known Asian dictator, who had been de-
throned, phoned us when he wanted to launch a
counteroffensive. He was about to storm the presidential palace, and he wanted a PR campaign to
back him up. More than Uzis or rocket launchers,
he knew that he needed the goodwill of the Western
democracies behind him. His record was clear enough
that we didn't want any part of it. We also get our
share of calls from Latin American narcomilitarists.

Irangate arms merchant Adnan Kashoggi wanted
help turning his image around in the United States.
A fugitive on tax evasion charges, trader Marc Rich
called me from Zug, Switzerland, wanting a reentry
plan that could ease him back into the States. The
Colombians have asked us to help spruce up their
image. We say no to them all. We did help the
Chileans during the grape poisoning scare, because
Chilean fruit is very important to the U.S. economy
and our winter fruit supply. Until recently, we would

not have helped Chile on a general political basis because of that government's human rights history.

It's not our place to mingle in the internal political affairs of other countries, especially where violence is involved. So, when two guys from Loureçio Marques in Mozambique came to see me asking for help in staging a coup d'état, I told them "We don't do coups."

A representative of the PLO tried to hire me in the early eighties, before the PLO moderated its stance. The fellow invited me to his hotel suite to have breakfast. No burnoose. No AK-47 rifle. He was dressed in a Western business suit and was very unexceptional, but for two things. First, I remember him pouring a small pot of coffee, a pitcher of cream, some salt, and a mound of sugar all on top of a bowl of shredded wheat. He lustily chomped through this mess while we talked. Second, he suggested that his PLO-manned contracting team would be a great labor source for building American embassies in the Middle East. I told him it was a very curious idea that would win no support in Washington. Remarkably, Uncle Sam did something just that bizarre when it used Soviet workers to build the bug-infested U.S. embassy in Moscow. Maybe that's where the PLO got the idea.

Perhaps my most colorful encounter with such intriguers was with Mafioso Michele Sindona. Sindona died several years ago in a Naples jail, allegedly of food poisoning. Insiders are sure it was a hit. Several years before he died, Sindona called me and invited me and a few of my associates to meet him for a drink. We knew Sindona by reputation, but we didn't know what he wanted. Sindona, after all, was no black-and-white case. Continental Bank of Illinois once had a partnership agreement with him when they bought into the Banca Privata Financieria in Milan. But, what was Sindona up to now? It could have been a campaign against world hunger or advice on how his associates could best own up to charges they faced. (Such straightforward or altruistic turns do happen, and it's hard to say no to them. I've known of ruthless Far Eastern real estate barons who suddenly decide to give millions to a cause like world literacy.)

So, on this frosty, sleeting January night in the 1970s, we went to Sindona's suite in the old Barclay Hotel in New York. It was about midnight and he and his associate invited us in. When we walked into the entryway, there was a silver tray loaded with perhaps twenty to twenty-five cordial glasses filled with vodka. After we tossed back a drink and an Italian coffee, Sindona looked across the room and said quietly that he wanted us to help spread legal gambling in the United States. Sindona wanted a national program. Meyer Lansky and his crowd had moved out of Cuba after Castro's ascendancy. Sindona had heard that the Lansky boys were going to mount a push for gambling throughout the United States, making Florida their beachhead.

I started to say to him, "Mr. Sindona, we just don't get involved in issues of that sort." He, however, cut me off midsentence with "Is there anybody giving you trouble? If there is, I can take care of them!" We protested, "No, no, there's nobody troubling us." But Sindona's mind had raced to its own conclusions. The only reason, he figured, we wouldn't take the business and the lavish fee it portended was because we were being either retained or threatened by one of his "competitors."

We left Sindona's suite soon afterward, and I can recall Sindona escorting us to the door with the words: "Remember, I can take care of them." Indeed, our meeting at the Barclay did not go unnoticed. No doubt the room was bugged or some lookout from a rival family was perched to see who went in and out of Sindona's suite. One of my colleagues at the meeting made the long drive home to Roslyn, New York, that night. When he was about to leave for work the next morning, he found all the tires on his car slashed. Later that morning, we got a mysterious call in the office, the anonymous, sinister voice vowing, "If you think that dealing with Michele Sindona is difficult now, the lesson your friend in Roslyn gets this morning will say how difficult it may be tomorrow." We never heard from either side again. New Jersey has become a gambling center ... and one hears rumors still about Detroit and Florida. I suspect that the biggest competitors have actually been revenue-hungry state governments that have been on a lottery rampage in recent years.

Our bout with the "families" was the most contested rivalry for our services I can remember. The incident points out how widely respected the power of skilled communicators is. Our response should make clear, I believe, that ethics must be the cornerstone of influence. And, that means projecting a strong ethical image. A shrewd communicator can fabricate a facade of ethics, but not for long.

Communications about ethics are not just symbolic. They are inseparable from the ethics of any organization. People's ethics are usually judged on the gap between what they say and what they do. As employees and observers compare actual conduct with the press releases and the on-camera interviews, they get an accurate idea of what the real ethical standards of the company are. I have never seen a truly unethical company elude being found out for long, especially these days. (In our trade, we learn about the likely ethics soft spots in a business before they become public knowledge.)

Bad ethics is bad for business. Those companies with questionable ethical practices will, in the least, find their attention drawn away from the business as they fight battles in the press and in the courts. They may even lose their very charter to do business. Scan the daily newspaper, and you will find countless examples of how ethics issues are stealing headlines:

Respected securities firm Drexel Burnham is slapped with the largest civil penalty in U.S. history and must ante up $650 million in fines to pay for admitted wrongdoings. Civil and criminal charges follow.

Financier Ivan Boesky is fined $100 million and carted off to the slammer. The soulmates of the great Wall Street scams become the cellmates of the morning after.

Former SEC Commissioner John Shad pledges $20 million to develop research and teaching in business ethics at the Harvard Business School. But educators doubt that much can be done to teach ethics to a worldly twenty-three-year-old.

More and more firms have adopted ethics codes, but codes are not guarantees. Consider the defense industry, which has some of the most stringent codes around, although some of its members have sold $3,000 coffeepots and $300 hammers to the Pentagon ... or have been embroiled in countless kickback schemes.

The growth of global business complicates ethics decisions. I meet with many business executives abroad. Once we get to know each other, they tell me they can't understand American righteousness. They don't understand why Americans expect that a globally uniform standard of values should exist. And, they ask, why especially should this standard be driven by U.S. administrative law rather than a time-honored religious or moral code? MIT Business School Dean Lester Thurow once said to me that this U.S. quest for universal standards stemmed from our "penchant to export U.S. ideology."

Crisis is a factor that dramatizes ethics issues and makes them even more complex. As chemical plants explode, airliners crash, products are tampered with, and potentially dangerous technology is sold to hostile powers, firms must confront serious ethical concerns—and not just as problems in crisis management.

Another way in which we have come to know ethics dilemmas, I'm sad to say, is through a very small number of clients. Sometimes, clients have asked us to help them do something wrong. I think that this situation arises with all kinds of professional services firms. For example, a client will ask us to pay for a set of luggage, an air ticket to Hawaii, or even a hooker and pad the amount of their firm's bill. Our people are given considerable training in ethics. For some people, an appeal to ethics just will not work. In this case, we have a strong, standard answer: "If you were ever caught, this would be terribly embarrassing for you . . . and we just couldn't allow you to put yourself in such a position." If we are asked a second time to do something shady, we confidentially advise the person's boss or resign the account.

So:

Make high ethical standards evident in everyday business decisions. Ethics cannot be allowed to be a separate realm of business life. Companies whose people get into ethics messes are like regular churchgoers who keep their Sunday services separate from their lives during the week. Unless you have experience in acting ethically on everyday business issues, you won't know how to act when a big challenge rolls around. Ethics must withstand the competition of meeting the monthly expense target or profit goal. Many companies deemphasize ethics unintentionally. Look at the rank most managers and companies give ethics among their corporate goals or standards. It's invariably last on a list of ten or twelve items—far away from the number-one goal of profit or return on investment. That sends a powerful message!

You hear much talk about gray areas, where there is allegedly no clear right or wrong, or employees are asked to do something against their conscience. I personally feel such cases are rare or nonexistent in those companies that communicate clear ethics standards. Problems generally begin when the employee has to guess what the company believes is right, or when the company is opportunistically vague about its standards. Some companies quietly encourage rule bending. If things go to the mat, however, they'll deny they ever encouraged such a thing.

Give employees clear ideas and symbols for what ethical behavior means. Yale law professor and ethics expert Geoffrey Hazard says, "The term *ethics* is used in so many different ways, it is difficult to know what is meant. Some believe being ethical means being in compliance with the law. Others use it to mean humane concerns." One thing is certain: "An ethical person is not someone who walks around with a beatific smile. Ethics reflect a serious concentration on getting the job done. If management sets the right example, you have the best chance to get ethical behavior." Professor Hazard summarizes that "If management deals in baloney, buck-passing and double-talk, employees learn 'that's the way they do things around here.' People behave according to their perception of the incentive structure."

The manager had better be a symbol of integrity in the company. Managers should always have in mind two or three examples when their personal ethics were tested and they triumphed. A manager should find occasions to relate these episodes, not for notoriety but because employees need symbolic behavior toward which they can aspire. They need tough, real-world situations where it would have been easy to concede and where they must not. At Hill and Knowlton, we always publicize inside the firm any business that we turn away because it doesn't meet our ethical standards or might represent a conflict. Last year, that kind of business totaled roughly $10 million. Our employees feel good about our company and its character when they know we turn away big business in the name of integrity.

Don't create codes of conduct and then expect them to *guarantee* ethical behavior. Most codes of conduct stress what the employee is prohibited from doing to the company, not what the company is forbidden to do to others. Codes may provide a basic framework, but they cannot replace a lively and continuous attention to ethics in making decisions. Ethics training per se may have marginal value, for people on the job as much as for business school students. Managers will be better off publicizing formally or informally how the company has responded to real-world ethical problems. One construction firm I know had extensive internal publicity on why it turned down a lucrative bridge-building contract, because it wouldn't pay the expected bribe. A beer distributor makes sure that the internal grapevine is "wired" to report the details at all levels when an employee is fired for internal theft. These are the "morality plays" that really open people's ears and eyes.

Don't equate ethical with legal behavior. There is a growing disparity between what's lawful and what's ethical. For one thing, it's harder and harder to know what the law is. Each day, the Commerce Clearing House sends lawyers a stack of papers a foot high. These are administrative law decisions that must be absorbed by the legal system and the companies. Presumably, these new rulings define ethical behavior. In fact, some of them do. But, we've gone far beyond the Ten Commandments. Few firms, if any, are in control of this avalanche of information. Lawyers are getting rich interpreting all the changes.

The way the system works ensures that there are countless companies in the country that break the law every day without knowing it. First, no company's general counsel can digest this kind of input. Redirecting it to and interpreting it for all of the company's increasingly decentralized operations is itself a full-time job for a legion of lawyers. Second, managers in Florida or South America or Indonesia may just choose to ignore the directives once they get them. It may take months for even the most scrupulous central monitoring to catch up with compliance breakdowns in the field.

I'm convinced that a smart team of investigators, dispatched by a congressional oversight committee, could take a pocketful of administrative law decisions and run a first-class witch-hunt. Firms would be nearly powerless to protect themselves.

This constant stream of new laws has other effects. Companies can no longer vigorously deny accusations of violating the law as automatically as they once did. When a company is accused of violating some obscure or recently enacted law, we counsel them to do the following: Affirm the company tries always to behave ethically. State that the company is investigating the charges immediately. And, sometimes, point out the massive volume of new laws and codes and rulings to which they are responding.

I think our legal system is actually damaging the ethical credibility of business. Companies are afraid of exposing themselves to litigation if they behave ethically. Let's say that a drug has long been approved for sale by the FDA. In continuing testing done by the manufacturer, it seems that the drug can actually be a carcinogen in certain cases. What should the pharmaceutical firm's first priority be? Getting the news out or protecting itself from a host of ambulance-chasing lawsuits?

Balance integrity and liability. I think we should worry as much about losing our integrity as we do about opening ourselves to legal liability. Torts and liability law are in a massive snarl in the United States. As much as anything, this snarl may contribute to business's perceived lack of ethics. According to Geoffrey Hazard, a firm with deep pockets "faces very complex choices. In trying to do the right thing, it can set itself up for legal attack. Large companies make attractive targets. In a world bristling with legal enforcement, it's hard for firms to operate with a conscience."

No manager can afford to ignore counsel's advice. But, if he heeds it blindly, he will pay for it in influence. He'll come across as suspicious and equivocating, scared of taking a stand. He won't own up to the obvious. Managers need to point out the good business reasons for taking a particular position. The attorneys may succeed in defending against a particular claim. But, the company can still suffer even greater losses in profits and market share because that winning defense costs goodwill and trust. Johns Manville, for example, let the asbestos issue get so far out of hand that the company was convicted before it was tried, and gave up the lion's share of its assets because it failed to communicate.

Fight the glamorization of unethical behavior. Values haven't changed, but the way in which they are reported has. Some suspicious souls have been turned into celebrities. They are the star guests at dinner and cocktail parties. As I read somewhere recently, "If you're indicted—you're invited." Some of you will remember how Tom Wolfe's book *Radical Chic* and *Mau-Mauing the Flak Catchers* scorned those Park Avenue matrons who entertained Black Panthers during the social activism of the seventies.

Many of the characters on the ethics stage in recent years look just like they walked off a Hollywood set. Entertainment television's grotesquely distorted view of business hasn't helped. Nor is it any surprise that a G. Gordon Liddy can strut from real life onto the sound stage of "Miami Vice" and be so believable. I think it's very important for the business community to "deglamorize" the white-collar criminal. I'm not talking about managers caught in impossible squeezes, who tried to do something ethical but were indicted on a legal technicality for a breach of administrative law. But when a manager has been tried and convicted, and it's clear that the manager was acting in his own selfish interests, he deserves to be pilloried, just like the drug dealer or the rapist. Businesspeople will get more credit for being ethical if they show that they are hard on their own.

Don't create incentives that cause the ethics problems you want to prevent. A leading ethics expert, Gary Edwards, Executive Director of the Ethics Resource Center in Washington, has portrayed the ethics problem in business poignantly: "Unethical behavior in large organizations involves good people. Your neighbors. Yourselves, perhaps. People who are down in the guts of the organization, who come to believe that in order to keep their job and do their job, they have to do what it takes. They're people who are stretched by management, by objectives that are beyond their ability to perform. They may work for years without feeling the pressure. But they wake up one day with objectives that perhaps they didn't set, or maybe they did and the market turned against them and they can't get there. And they've got two kids in college and a mortgage. And they look around for signals about what to do. And the organization gives signals that it doesn't intend to give. They look around, and what they see is that people who meet quarterly profit performance objectives go up the ladder. And people who don't, get plateaued or they're gone." American businesspeople—business leaders especially —are believed to be more concerned over hearing about ethical violations than about having them. Only the manager who actively wants to know about trouble will earn credibility. Only the manager who refuses to "wink" at offenses can hope to sustain ethical behavior in his work group.

6

The CEO's Circle

Influence at the CEO's level is a complex game for very high stakes. In fighting his way to the top, the newly named CEO has proven his ability to influence the people of his company. He has shown a grasp of influence in the marketplace and has likely tangled with government and special interests. Next, he must exert influence in his new peer group—among other CEOs. This agenda covers different territory. He must deal with Wall Street and face the perpetual risk of takeover or reorganization. He must be the corporate citizen who raises money for the community and makes company contributions to causes and institutions. He is the political benefactor, backing key officials vital to his firm's interests. He is his company's access to a network of powerful people throughout the country. And, he is the global executive who must understand how to wield influence in foreign capitals.

The lessons in this chapter have special relevance to the CEO, but I think they are also very important to anyone who aspires to top management. Influence at the CEO level has a great deal to do with values and perspective. People get to be CEOs partly because they have the right values and they use the power triangle. They communicate, see that their communication is recognized, and convert that recognition into influence. They know how to operate with the proper style.

Show your stature in the right ways. People in powerful positions can be remarkably vain and petty. Some of them are very insecure and must constantly prove to others that they have influence. When the funeral of Emperor Hirohito took place in Japan, we were approached by many Third World countries who wanted to upgrade their place in line for the ceremonies. It was silly. Often, there are events that bring together many top executives in Washington at the same time. It may be a dinner sponsored by the Trilateral Commission or the Conference Board or some other prestigious organization. I can't tell you how many calls I've had over the years asking me to intervene so that someone's private plane would be first on the runway to leave the next morning. It doesn't mean a thing.

I'll never forget attending a small lunch for Australian Prime Minister Bob Hawke. The group included eleven CEOs, Hawke, and myself. General Motors' Roger Smith said over dessert that he had to "make three more cities" that day and needed to leave. I was embarrassed, and I'm sure others were too. The irony was that while Smith left early, his chauffeur was stuck waiting in jammed traffic behind the limos of seven of the other CEOs. He was still sitting in his car as the rest of us came out from the lunch.

In contrast, there are other executives who know how to assert their status in low-key but effective ways. Brewster Atwater at General Mills and Mike Miles at Kraft General Foods quietly labor on policy committees for organizations like the Business Roundtable. They are exerting meaningful influence and advancing the agenda for business. It's not the takeoff slot on the tarmac but the position on the lead committees that matters.

Jim Bere, Borg Warner's CEO, is a very powerful community supporter in Chicago. He doesn't seek out visible praise, but he gets things done. Of all the industrial leaders in Chicago, he's one of the best friends of the community. He has the natural altruism and sense of vision that would make a good U.S. president.

Associate with groups that will give you insight and contacts. Major company CEOs have an inviting array of memberships from which to choose. They include such important forums as the Trilateral Commission, the Conference Board, and the Business Roundtable. There are also exclusive symposiums such as Davos in Switzerland and Bohemian Grove in San Francisco. There is the Investor Relations conference in Florida each December and conferences that *Fortune* sponsors throughout the year.

These are all opportunities for CEOs to showcase themselves and make substantive statements that can shape industrial and national policy. They also give exposure. I know CEOs who go to nearly all of these events. I know others who attend nearly none. Both make mistakes. The critical issue is first to identify your agenda. Figure out the people you need to meet, the ideas you want to advance, and the developmental experiences that could help you most. Then create a plan.

Build contacts for pragmatic reasons. What good does it do to influence your peers? There are three very sound, practical reasons to build peer contacts at the CEO level. First, you could find customers for your goods and services. Second, that is the network you will have built should lightning strike. You never know when you'll need a white knight to save you from a raider or when you'll have to unload a division. Third, you must belong to the club, to the council of lords. In your community and with your management, your CEO status will be validated if you just supped with John Akers of IBM. It would also be very hard to have dinner with Akers and not learn some pretty valuable insights into management.

If you're a small-company CEO, be prepared to work harder for access. At the U.S.–Japan Business Conference, the little guy is treated like wallpaper, unless he can come up with viewpoints and comments that declare he's exceptional. How does the little guy deal with it? He goes to his management consultant or outside advisor and makes a withdrawal from his Favor Bank account. He says, "I want your help preparing position papers, giving me statistical information, training me, doing whatever it takes to position me."

The small-company CEO should also work closely with the professional staff that supports heavyweight management forums. The professional staff has some control over the agenda of meetings. They may be able to steer a topic onto an agenda where the CEO has expertise, where perhaps he could participate in a panel discussion. The top twenty CEOs have star power, but the staff has a say on how the seating charts for dinner tables are drawn. They can put you on the dais or on the right committee. CEOs and top managers should deal with these staffs. This is not something you delegate to your secretary—because this sends a signal as to what level you think the staff is on. Bring the staff person up to your level.

Recognize that the CEO's circle is a recruiting network. Peter Drucker said recently that more and more CEOs of small companies will be recruited to run large companies. The management ranks have become so lean that there are few opportunities to gain the experience needed to be a big-company CEO. Consequently, more CEOs will be plucked out of small companies. The "junior" CEOs who conduct themselves well in the circle have the best chances to advance.

Part II

BECOMING THE INFLUENTIAL MANAGER

7

The First 100 Days

As Franklin Roosevelt and his advisors knew so well, the first 100 days are the most critical. Any good manager understands that early impressions are lasting impressions. Roosevelt knew this when he became president in the depths of the Great Depression. His first three months witnessed the advent of many new social and economic programs, plus a series of significant governmental appointments, and the declaration of a bank holiday.

Lee Iacocca, another "president," also understood the importance of the first 100 days as the time to identify the essential problems and to begin solving them. He did this brilliantly at Chrysler, where he forged a partnership with the government as he drew up plans for the bailout. He created a solid relationship with his ad agency Kenyon and Eckhardt as well as with Doug Fraser of the United Auto Workers Union (by putting him on Chrysler's board of directors). He mobilized his troops from and in every corner.

As he takes over the giant Pillsbury, Ian Martin of Grand Met is making things happen and he's doing it in a thoughtful way. For starters, he's bought a house in Minneapolis, and is actually living in it, which is a clear demonstration of his commitment. He also started holding meetings in Minneapolis, had his firm donate money to the community, and built relationships with the local press.

A promotion or a position in a new company is an excellent time to launch and influence a program. You can leverage the newness and control a great many perceptions people will have of you. I have seen plenty of managers at top levels as they began new jobs. That's because I'm often involved in announcing their appointments and mapping out their strategy with the press. In the first few days, and often sooner, I can tell if a manager is headed for trouble. It boils down to his ability to take himself seriously in the right way. If he takes himself too seriously—if he's pompous, an egomaniac, or blindly goal driven—he's headed for trouble. What I look for is someone who is balanced, intense, and thoughtful. The properly serious manager will have a plan, an agenda to exert influence.

When you receive a promotion or join a new company, you want to have as much input into the announcement as you can. Most managers entering a new job will have the appointment reported in a written internal announcement and most often in an announcement to the press. For a junior-level manager, these announcements are usually routine. If you try to insist on special announcement treatment as a low-ranking manager, most companies will think you're making a fool of yourself. Announcing changes of power is a carefully controlled ceremony with profound nuances, especially in corporations.

As you go up the organization, announcements carry considerably more weight. They can signal, among other things, a company's change in attitude, the new role of a particular department, or a change of authority for your job. For managers, middle-level and up, the announcement is an advertisement of coming attractions. People are going to read and study it with great care. By all means, ask to review the announcement about your appointment before it's released. Here are some considerations you should have in mind when you read your announcement draft:

Don't be trapped by an announcement that overpromises change. Does the announcement say that you are going to introduce change? If so, how much change, of what sort, and how fast? Who in the company is likely to be threatened by the change? Who will be encouraged by it? Does it set an expectation against which you will be measured in six months or a year? Make sure that any unrealistic expectations are not included.

Announce change with realism. Argue for the most realistic announcement. The announcement should also be bullish about the future and positive about the way it reaches out to rivals. Change is potent medicine. Don't build up resistance to it in advance. It won't help you get the job done if your announcement is a declaration of war or a boast that others will want to prove wrong.

Treat your predecessor in terms of *your* future needs. Is he leaving voluntarily? Going to a better assignment? Is it implied that he failed at his job? Some managers want the announcement to smite the predecessor who failed. There's no benefit in doing this. The organization will know what is happening, and, in cases of actual wrongdoing, it's much better to let a person leave with dignity unless corruption or criminality is involved. If a negative comment is in order, the lawyers should be closely involved in drafting the wording.

Make sure your authority is clear. A common problem is that people are promised the authority to "really shake things up," but the announcement sharply qualifies the amount of shaking up they are going to be permitted. Your authority almost always grows at someone else's expense. It's a lot easier to tell people that they are now more important or that their power remains unchanged than to tell them that they have lost authority. Make sure the announcement is direct about how power is being realigned, but not gloating or cruel.

Use the announcement to create alliances with adversaries. Let's say that you're appointed the head of global marketing. Responsibility for worldwide product distribution has just been centralized with you, which means that the executive vice-president of international operations, who manages nine territory managers, has just lost turf, and so have his people. The announcement about you should include a statement from the executive vice-president that this change is positive and that he and his people are committed to making it work.

Closely control the timing of announcements. Employees who read about company changes for the first time in the newspapers, or who hear about them initially from outside sources, feel betrayed. At the very least, they should get the word the same time the press does. I have, for example, heard of countless plant closings at which employees first heard the information from a news reporter who shoved a microphone in front of the worker's face and asked him how he felt about losing his job. Every important announcement of a personnel appointment or change for a work unit needs a written timing and action program. Usually that plan is just a page long. However, when a major oil company asked us to coordinate the announcement and introduction of its new CEO, the move was backed with a carefully engineered,

60-page action manual. Often we are brought in six months or a year before a major management change is made. Advance planning can be that essential.

Consider what your appointment means for the press. One of the great paradoxes of business life is that announcements are extremely important inside an organization . . . and relatively unimportant to the press. Inside an organization, you usually have to be at the manager or director level for the inside announcement to say something tailor-made about your appointment. For the press, you generally have to be an officer or senior officer for there to be much interest. It's never too early, nonetheless, to study how management heavyweights think about the press when they move into a new job.

For a typical new appointment, here's how we counsel an executive to prepare himself:

Ask your communications department for a list of the key reporters who will follow this announcement.

If you are expected to give an interview, request recent articles that a reporter may have written about the company or the industry.

Make sure that you clear with your communications department any conversation you intend to have with a reporter *before* you have it.

If your appointment has material importance for your firm, or implies a change in direction, ask if any effort is being made to line up endorsements from analysts or industry experts. (Reporters don't rely on a firm's news releases when they praise or pan a change. They go to outside experts. Smart executives will have built positive relationships with industry authorities long before they are needed.)

When talking with the press, don't commit to major changes in the business until you have had a chance to study the situation. This is especially true if you are new to the company. (Generally, it's better to talk about major changes *after* they have been implemented, not before.)

Ask reporters for input on how they see the industry and its strategic challenges. (Not only can you learn valuable information but it demonstrates that you are a listener.)

Offer to talk to reporters in the future, either for quotation or off the record, as appropriate, for roundups or feature pieces on your industry. (Make sure that your communications department approves and always keep the department in the loop each time there's a contact with the press.)

Act early. It's my experience that what a manager does in the first days of a new job has great bearing on how he is perceived long afterward. A major career change is the perfect time to launch a personal influence program. When you make a career move, people are already expecting to see you differently. Use the event to your advantage.

It doesn't hurt to have some early successes. After three weeks on the job, maybe you find a great way to shave travel expenses and you publicize it in a low-key update at your next departmental staff meeting. Maybe you reduce the number of unproductive meetings or needless reports. Perhaps you hang on to a key rival who everyone was sure would walk when you got your new job. Make sure that management is updated on the challenge you faced in keeping this person and how pleased you were that he decided to stay.

Make commitment carefully. It's a common occurrence: The newly appointed manager pledges to get into the field and "meet everyone." He vows to get direct input from all parts of the company to solve problems in his area. He promises to meet with key suppliers and customers. A year later, he's still walled in his office filling out reports, having convinced people throughout the company that he is "just like the rest of them."

Maybe time and budget limits permit you to hit only two or three company facilities. But you can certainly refer to those visits in memos or notes and call attention to the effort you are making to get input. If you can, try to hold a session or two with rank-and-file personnel when you visit a remote location. Call one employee a day on his birthday or his service anniversary. Look for issues that can create a communications chain back to these people. You are about to change the benefit plan or launch a new work procedure. Call up the long-timer on the assembly line in Seattle or the auditor in Santa Fe. Get their views by framing a "What if . . ." (provided the pending change doesn't have burning sensitivity). With modest effort, you can create contact loops such as these throughout the company. It will get you noticed and give you positive power.

Being able to call just a few employees in a remote state or a foreign country *by name* will magnify your apparent influence in the company. It also creates a valuable feedback source for you to feel the pulse of the company. Some managers seem to know "everybody." My experience is that almost no one really does. Some skilled managers create the impression that they are at least in touch. To stay on equal footing, you should, too. The key is to amplify what you do so that your leadership is recognized.

8

The New–and More Influential –You

Many managers feign modesty. Don't imitate them. They always say, "My people really deserve the credit." Don't believe them. If you want to be influential, you have to step forward without being pushy.

You can't pretend you are less than you really are. Carefully and diplomatically, you must make sure your influence is recognized. If you don't, you won't be heard in Washington, or anywhere else. You won't be listened to when your company needs the ear of its trade association. Community and industry participation is not something to be taken lightly. Being influential is something you owe your industry, your community, your company, and yourself.

Jim Bere, the CEO of Borg Warner, has a favorite saying: "Any executive has three marriages—to his spouse, to his job, and to his community." For any manager at any stage, balance is key.

I recall talking to Bob Abboud when he was CEO of First Chicago. He had been looking at the résumés of various executives. As he scanned them, he said, "This guy spends too much time in the community. This guy is about right. This guy doesn't spend enough." CEOs want managers who make a balanced commitment to their communities.

Not long ago I was interviewing a man who wanted a job at Hill and Knowlton. He was clearly well qualified, and his résumé was impressive. But still I had reservations, in large part because three pages of his résumé were devoted to listing what he was doing for the community. "Dave," I said to him, "what's in all of these activities for Hill and Knowlton?" He replied that they lead to contacts that could lead to business. "That would make me happy," I said, "but your main job would be to do business, not just to find it. And while we do want you to give something back to the community, your job here would be to serve clients. If you can squeeze these three pages down to a third of a page, you can have the job." He did and we hired him.

There are many different leadership styles, many ways to realize an agenda, to exert influence. Over the years, I have identified certain characteristics common to all influential leaders. Here's what to do:

Focus your energies. Prioritization is one of the hardest jobs in management. It is particularly hard for the perfectionist. For that kind of person, everything has to be done, and it all has to be done at once. This problem bedeviled President Jimmy Carter particularly. Hedrick Smith, in his masterful study of Washington politics titled *The Power Game*, writes: "Carter always had so many priorities that he seemed to have none. He suffered from what political scientist James Mac-Gregor Burns called 'strategic myopia.'" According to Warren Bennis and Burt Nahus, a Carter cabinet member compared

Carter's perspective to looking at the wrong side of a tapestry. I suspect that's why the Carter agenda was so often accused of having so much detail and so little focus.

You can always "read" an effective manager's priorities in what he does and what he says. The manager's priorities are clear symbols for others in an organization to follow.

Declare victory. A manager in a new position should always look for opportunities to declare victory. If your boss has a weekly activity report, find a way to mention the fine work of your subordinates. If your people are about to solve a genuinely tough problem, let management know that the problem is a real "bear." Update your bosses periodically. Then, when you finally lick the problem, they can share in the win.

Declaring victory is also important for firms. If you're the underdog gaining ground, you have to let your employees, your suppliers, your bankers, and others know you are moving ahead. Maybe it's an article in the trade press or the local papers. Maybe a rating agency upgrades the valuation of your commercial paper, and you send copies of the letter with a handwritten note to all of your managers saying, "Let's make this good news give us even more momentum!"

Both firms and individuals should look at the list of important things you must achieve in the next six to twelve months. Perhaps there are ten or fifteen items on the list. Take the three or four that are easy to achieve, complete them, and then get the message out that you are on a roll. Such action will often turn momentum to your side.

Bestow honor carefully. Companies must be very careful about how they bestow honor. Notoriety can become infamy. In the southern states, utility companies took to naming nuclear power plants after retired executives before these plants were ever fueled and running. Now, they sit—useless mausoleums—still bearing such names as Hatch and Vogel.

So now the names of legendary executives in the utilities industries are associated with multimillion-dollar boondoggles that are lying fallow in the middle of backwater swamps.

Companies are always creating totems and legends. Look at what the Ford family did to Edsel Ford. They wanted to honor a family legend, so they put his name on a car, and it failed miserably! Thirty years later, despite Edsel Ford's outstanding success at his company, the word *Edsel* represents a big-scale marketing idea that bombed!

Make change an ally. Management experts say today's adaptive company is likely to experience significant organizational change each six to twelve months. Change threatens. It is also unavoidable. So, you better be on the side of change, and you need to show your people how change is on their side. It's up to any manager to interpret change for his people. Your job is to pick out the important risks and worries in key changes and determine how you'll neutralize them. Your job is also to find the opportunities in change—to make sure they come true and to publicize them.

Make change positive, bold, and promising. Above all, point out how any change actually benefits employees. Explain how the failure to change a particular practice will make the company less competitive. Without change, the company's financial strength and people's jobs are threatened. Point out that the adaptable people are the ones who are promoted. Show that the growing divisions are the ones that have mastered change.

Pin on medals for small achievements as well as big ones. Jim Bere at Borg Warner and Bill Smithburg at Quaker Oats are great at this. So much in business rests on getting the little things right. When our monthly "President's Report" goes out at Hill and Knowlton, it's always referring to a secretary who sacrificed a weekend typing to help win a proxy fight or some intrepid soul setting up a satellite dish in Rangoon for a global press conference.

Empower the total organization. Henry Schacht, the CEO of Cummins Engine, will take ten to fifteen calls a day from the "little people" in his company, because he knows that they aren't little at all. He listens to their beefs and suggestions and he tries to act on them. It's his way of energizing the organization. It's also one of the reasons why Cummins has such superb operational management. It's especially important to showcase successful entrepreneurial suggestions discovered this way. I've seen this practice vitalize the entire attitude of a company.

Tell stories as a teacher would.* Ronald Reagan is a great example of the master storyteller. What made him so effective is that the stories were always sharply polished to prove a point. There is another very basic link between storytelling and influence. Influential people are supposed to live interesting lives. Fresh, lively "war stories" interweave you with important events and people. They prove your life is interesting, but—obviously—the stories must also be true.

Many influential folks deny that they read *People* magazine, and many don't. Still, I've known very few influential individuals who didn't create their own version of *People* in their daily conversations. Everybody wants to know the hot news from the financial centers, the real "scoop" on Bill Agee and Mary Cunningham, how Margaret Thatcher and François Mitterrand get along at state dinners, and what Ralph Nader's next cause is going to be.

---

*This is a point also made by Tom Peters in his valuable study *Thriving on Chaos*. On several points, the reader will see an affinity between my recommendations and Peters' ideas. He has stimulated my thinking many times.

Measurement is the beginning point for any thoughtful plan to increase influence. You must begin by understanding in what direction your influence is moving. Are you already progressing around the power triangle, or is your influence on the ebb? Here are some tips on how to measure the direction of your personal influence:

Learn to recognize when your influence is growing. A surprising number of managers fail to answer the "call." Managers are often tested to see if they are ready and willing to exercise influence. Some signals to watch for follow:

You are asked to reconcile a dispute between departments.

A younger manager needs a mentor and you are recommended to take this person "under your wing."

Your industry's trade association can't resolve the right standards for a key product, and your boss wants you to take the lead for your company.

A crisis happens, and you are asked to help reassure others in your work unit that the company is doing everything possible to resolve it.

Know when your influence is shrinking. Companies are equally clear in telegraphing when a manager's influence is shrinking. Suddenly, he's taken off the "short list" for important internal communications, and his attendance is no longer viewed as necessary at key operating meetings. He's moved out of the executive suite "so that he can be closer to his people." A feature story showcases seven other managers on his level, but not him.

Just as managers can be "tested" when their influence is on the rise, they can be "set up" when their influence is on the decline. As I said earlier, whenever you are given a special assignment, your first thought should be "Can I succeed?" If a situation feels wrong, your next question should be "Am I being nudged into failure?"

A manager should grow wary when a controversial issue comes up and he hears, "Joe, you take this one." Watch for the signals:

No one else wants to touch it.

Others have tried to solve the problem and have damaged themselves in the process.

It's a sticky puzzle, but smaller in status than others you have already solved.

The suggestion comes on the heel of some other failure in your performance.

The person suggesting you be brave has something to gain if you fail.

Know, too, when your influence status is undecided. I was once making a pitch for business to a group of very influential CEOs. They were the board of a trade association and we were competing against three other large agencies for the account. I knew one of the directors very well. At a reception given before the competing presentations were made, I kept walking up to my acquaintance to say hello. He kept bouncing away from me like a ricocheting bullet. Finally, I cornered him, and asked quietly, "Bill, why are you walking away?" He responded, "Well, I don't want to be tagged as close to somebody who might lose."

———

Influence is a relative term. Managers are influential only in the context of other people and organizations. As times and conditions change, they internalize the key questions they must keep asking themselves. Focus on these benchmarks:

Use your influence as much as your authority. Horst Schroeder, the former president of Kellogg, is a great example of a manager who uses influence rather than authority to get things done. He works through networks. He coaches. He never orders; he always asks. He's a "billiards communicator." He bounces it off the cushion every time. Insecure managers and bureaucrats lean on their authority. Shrewd managers use persuasion and positioning.

Maintain parity in your industry. In any city, you immediately know the people and companies who are the yardstick for influence and stature. In New York, it's organizations like Morgan Stanley. In Chicago, First Chicago and Allstate set the pace. In California, things are a little different. There, the Japanese have coalesced into a quiet industrial power that is really the first tier, and they are setting the style of influence in that state. You see their tremendous power when they are able to beat back issues such as unitary taxation. In California, you have to measure yourself against the Japanese. Always know who's at the head of the line and where you stand in relation to them.

Associate with the right outside organizations. This concern becomes more and more important the further one advances in management. A person's influence is often extrapolated from his community associations. There are a few simple guideposts that can help any executive view that challenge in the proper light.

Only involve yourself with projects that deliver recognizable impact. Being yet another faceless volunteer worker for the Red Cross or the United Way may do your heart good and it may add a line to your résumé, but it won't have any value for your power credentials. Find a project with which you can be personally identified. Solve a tough problem that has stymied everyone else in the community. Prove your leadership in the community if you haven't yet been given the charge to prove it in your company.

I have seen many hard-charging junior executives who grabbed on to a special campaign or a drive to raise funds for a new ward of a local hospital. They took the initiative, and it got them noticed fast. Provided a person is doing his basic job well, community involvement can be a potent edge. A reputation for successful community project work can catapult the junior executive close to important senior business leaders. Active top managers are constantly on the lookout for good organizers who can get results from a volunteer team. I have seen cases where managers actually have been recruited away to another firm because they caught a senior manager's eye through voluntary work.

Set a style for your community efforts: tenacious, energetic, low-key, but visible enough to be noticed. The best top managers master that balance.

Grow your community involvements along with your career. Some managers stay tied to very small community programs even after they have rapidly advanced. Sometimes, these associations are nostalgic retreats into the past, for example, a scout troop or the board of a small charity. The fact is that the executive owes society more, and it's expected he will involve himself at the highest level of which he is capable. His career standing sets his social and trade association involvements and vice versa. An executive who wants to maximize his influence will avoid any dissonance: A CEO with the leading firm in a community belongs on the board of the largest—and presumably strongest—bank in the city. He should be a director of the most important charities. He should be heading the leading fund-raising drives.

Always serve your customer's values first. This is especially true for the small businessperson. It's surprising how many managers overlook the importance of doing this. If I sell to the trade, who are my two or three most important customers? What community activities are most important to them? If I sell to the general public, what concerns and priorities are important to them? The smart executive will make these real factors in deciding on community organization and project involvement. Mary Kay Cosmetics, for example, contributes both money and leadership time to the fight against breast cancer. A number of food companies are involved in public campaigns to combat hunger and improve nutrition.

Be heard in the right circle. Look at managers of comparable companies in your communities or similar companies in your own industry. What kinds of speeches are they giving and to what audiences? Are they invited into meaningful civic and industry forums? Are they testifying in Washington and in state capitals on key issues? Then ask yourself, How do I compare?

9

What to Do When the Trick Is on You

In the spring of 1987, just as I was set to fulfill the fondest (temporal) dream of any Catholic and meet with the Pope—at his summer residence, Castle Gondolfo, no less—Italy's leading business weekly, *Il Mondo*, ran a story "exposing" my Gorbachev connection. (This was long before the Pope's historic meeting with Gorbachev in 1989.)

According to an anonymous source, I was the gray eminence behind *Glasnost!* Of course, the story was completely false, but its very appearance in *Il Mondo* was to scuttle my meeting with the Pope. After all, how would it look for the Pope to be asking the advice of someone who had also counseled Gorbachev?

So, without the expert advice of R. Dilenschneider, the Holy Father went ahead with the 1987 trip to the United States, and the trip turned out to be a logistical nightmare wholly unworthy of the prelate.

About a year later, I was returning from Switzerland, where I'd taken part in the World Economic

Forum, an annual gathering at which world business and political leaders assemble to help set an agenda of important issues. I had been asked by the Italian press to hold a news conference in Milan on my way back to the States, and there were about sixty reporters there. *La Repubblica, La Stampa,* and all the others attended, including my friends from *Il Mondo.*

About fifteen minutes into the press conference, while I was making my opening statements, without warning a man I had never seen before marched to the front of the room. Short, bullet-headed, red-haired, with very Slavic features, he positioned himself between me and the press without so much as glancing at me. Addressing them in flawless Italian, he said his name was Alexander Valgin, and that he represented the Ministry of Culture of Russian Federations. He went on to say that he was pleased that "Bob" Dilenschneider was in Italy, because he had just received special authorization from Soviet "cultural organizations" (a term I understood to mean the government) to provide Hill and Knowlton with Russian art treasures to be distributed around the world. He described some of the objects as icons, triptyches, "magnificent" lacquered plates, and samovars. And then, as abruptly as he had started, Valgin smiled, and spying an empty seat in the crowd, sat down.

I went on with the press conference. When I was asked the inevitable question, I said I had absolutely nothing to do with Comrade Valgin, and no knowledge of why he had introduced himself to the conference in such a novel way. I explained that I had never met him and knew nothing about him or his organization. Eventually, the topics shifted to Davos, American views on takeovers in Italy, and how the domestic Italian auto industry would be affected by increased competition.

Later, in the hallway, Valgin accosted me, and beckoned me to sit down with him. Furtively, he opened a huge valise, from which tumbled hundreds of single sheets of paper, all in Cyrillic script, all addressed "To Whom It May Concern," from different Soviet cultural institutions, saying that their artifacts and art objects were available (for good hard Western currency) to anyone reading the letter.

His intention, Valgin swore, was not to sell the artifacts but to "allow" Hill and Knowlton's worldwide network to exhibit these treasures. Our clients would earn "tremendous prestige" from being associated with these fine Soviet—that is to say, Czarist and almost all Christian—works of art. Allegedly, I was the first Westerner in decades to be offered the opportunity to be a Russian art impresario. All this spawned by the new world of *Glasnost!*

A small warning bell began to ring in my mind. And when Valgin volunteered, "I want you to know I'm not political," an assurance he repeated about three times in the next two minutes, the warning bell clanged. I remembered Emerson's observation: "The louder he talked of his honor, the faster we counted our spoons." An instant later my suspicions were confirmed when Valgin interjected, dryly, "I want a million dollars."

Thus, in two probably unrelated acts of mischief, I had been had twice, and both times the Soviets were involved. When I searched for motive, some things became clear to me. We had been in negotiations with people in Moscow for some time about opening a Hill and Knowlton office there. The more we studied the idea, however, the less enthused we were. At first it had seemed "glamorous" to be in the Eastern bloc, but eventually we learned that it was going to be a very slow and unprofitable road, and our firm had cooled on the idea. I suspect the Soviets were not happy about our change of heart. I think they were trying, in a clumsy kind of way, to force our hand with the stunts. It was never clear to me whether Valgin had personally decided on this tactic or whether the Soviets officially were behind it.

These two events point out three important lessons on how to deal with dirty tricks in the halls of influence:

First, deny false allegations forcefully. I certainly denied the contention that I worked for Gorbachev. But because I found it to be more amusing than serious, my denials were more joking than grave. The two events were not perpetrated by the same plotter. Still, the first enabled the second to happen. I had not considered that the Gorbachev allegation was very serious business in Italy where plenty of real communists walk the streets. My not giving it a strong enough denial let the Soviets see my amusement as a kind of invitation to move in on me.

Second, when you suspect someone is out to "get you," control your exposure. I should never have walked into a Milan press conference without better information on who would be attending, especially with the previous to-do in Italy. No serious member of the Italian press believed these events to be anything more than silly coincidences, but in my trips to Italy immediately thereafter, I shunned large gatherings. I was very careful not to publicize my itinerary and plans, and emphasized to the various parties with whom I met privately the absurdity of these alleged connections with the Soviets.

Third, recognize that dirty tricks are now an international business. You can do everything right as far as your U.S. constituencies are concerned, and still be undermined abroad. There was once an etiquette that protected foreigners. Now, business is business . . . and business is also global. That's the lesson my experiences in Milan drove home to me.

———

Some of the dirty tricks I've seen in business have been remarkably blatant. Dick Hyde—a Hill and Knowlton executive—and I were meeting one day with a Pittsburgh lawyer named Howard Swartz at the William Penn Motor Inn in Harrisburg. We were discussing a very sensitive piece of legislation pending in the Pennsylvania House, when there was a knock at the door. In came a man in coveralls with an electrician's belt, who said he was "replacing TVs." We told him to skip us, that we were having a meeting and wouldn't be watching any TV, but he kept on insisting. We stood firm and told him to get lost. Finally, he turned away, exasperated. We carried on with our meeting, broke for dinner, and then came back to the room to continue our talks. As we walked through the lobby, we saw this same character heading out the door of the motel. This time he was wearing a different-colored set of coveralls with the name of a florist embroidered on the back! We got back to the room and found a huge bouquet of roses on the dresser, with a gift card from some fictitious trade association. Of course, affixed to one of the stems was a bug, and not the crawling kind. It doesn't take a genius to figure out the moral of the story: If things look fishy, they probably are.

Not all dirty tricks are the same, but here are a few other tips that I think are helpful in guarding against some common ones:

When unknown people call you, never assume that they are who they say they are. Call them back, preferably through the central number of the publications or the firm they say they're working for. Some enterprising reporters will try to pass themselves off as remote office managers of your own company trying to get inside data on a company crisis that just happened. There are also stock arbitragers who will claim to be reporters for prestigious business publications simply to get managers to talk with them. They want to pry loose an important piece of inside data that the press may not be onto yet.

In April 1989, trading in IBM's stock was stopped because of a prank call. Thanks to fast work by the New York Stock Exchange, trading quickly resumed. Had the NYSE staff not been trained to identify crank calls, the prank could have sent the entire market into a nosedive. Dirty tricks can make big waves, and no one is immune.

Always be slow in bringing people along the "trust curve." I know of firms that have sent spies to work in other companies. Months later, these counteragents bolt back to their original employers with a host of secrets. This cheap trick is often used in politics where an insider from one camp will defect to a new candidate, only to be swayed back by a "call of conscience" . . . after he has gleaned enough inside information.

Learn that most dirty tricks are just lies contrived at your expense. The most common kind of dirty trick is simply stretching the truth. For example, some reporters will tell you that your boss has given you permission to talk with this paper openly on any issue. Special-interest group leaders will tell the press that they have your full support. (In reality, you support them only on a single issue.) Your company lobbyist backs a senator totally, rather than just on the designated issue to which you agreed. (The lobbyist wants a post on the senator's staff.) This kind of abuse goes on constantly. And, the only protection is management awareness and vigilance.

WHAT TO DO WHEN THE TRICK IS ON YOU

When dealing with colleagues who play dirty tricks, here's a defense gambit I read about once: Let's say a peer keeps pirating your ideas. Write that person a note saying, "I'm flattered that you found my suggestions on changing the warehouse inventory system so workable. You are doubtless the right person to do the implementation. Let me know if I can be of help down the road." Then, send copies to your boss and his. There are many other ways to ensure that the gold stars go on the right foreheads. Once you've practiced "success sharing," the right reflexes become downright easy.

If you try to exert influence, expect that there will always be forces conniving to take that influence away from you. Opponents will play dirty tricks. These tricks can sabotage your agenda. You better learn to spot them, defuse them, and prevent them.

10

Use Your Symbolic Role

Susan Eisenhower of the Eisenhower Group, who is an advisor to us, travels frequently to the Soviet Union. In doing so, she has become something of an expert on symbolic change. There's hardly a better place for studying the symbolism of leadership changes. For example, look at how Gorbachev "zapped" former Premier Brezhnev. In 1988, the Brezhnev subway stop was renamed, and the commemorative plaque was peeled off the apartment house where Brezhnev once lived.

Susan Eisenhower finds the treatment of Brezhnev rather disquieting because it reflects the old ways, not the innovations that have become the Gorbachev trademark. "The impulse to eradicate the image and presence of the Brezhnev leadership is not really 'new thinking,'" says Susan. I agree. It's no great reform that they have renamed the Brezhnev memorials. Purging is old-fashioned Soviet thinking. The real reform would have been if they *hadn't* purged Brezhnev out of the system.

Eisenhower explains further, "Gorbachev strikes us dramatically because he is different from our traditional view of the Soviet leadership. He departs from the stereotype." In my opinion, we are grateful for what Gorbachev is saying. If you study his positions, Susan suggests, "It is most interesting the extent to which Gorbachev's concepts and proposals echo the American rhetoric of the fifties ... his approach sounds surprisingly familiar and comforting." Gorbachev is departing from the past at the same time he echoes our past. He's playing Golden Oldies, and while we can't always name the tune, we do recognize the melody.

The influential manager is one who knows the value of, and how to use, his symbols for maximum effectiveness.

Symbolize deep commitment to your customers. Symbolic involvement is essential. The art of ritual delegation shows that the CEO at least handled the issue, but sometimes the CEO can't simply coordinate. He must personally involve himself, especially if he wants something special from a supplier or customer. I am reminded of a recent business pilgrimage. Sears is several times the size of Montgomery Ward. According to the *Wall Street Journal,* both retailers wanted the Maytag appliance line. Ward's CEO visited Maytag's headquarters in Newton, Iowa. Sears' CEO did not. Ward's got the Maytag line; Sears didn't. If this personal involvement success is true for CEOs, you better believe it will be true down the entire marketing chain of command.

Teach by action. Consider this story about Cray Computer. The firm's founder, Seymour Cray, used to build a sailboat each spring and sail it through to the fall. In autumn, he would burn the boat. Cray's actions had a message for his employees: What worked before might not work again. The cartoonist Rube Goldberg was equally symbolic. He would give away everything he owned every two years. Fred Smith—

using Navy flag language for "a job well done"—sends "BRAVO/ZULU" stickers to Federal Express employees who have excelled as a way of saying "good work!" The stickers are often accompanied by a small check or other reward. When Jim Burke was Johnson & Johnson's CEO, he gave positive recognition to managers who took legitimate risks, even when they failed. These kinds of symbolic actions will inspire people faster and better than any long-winded speech ever could. Therefore they are superior communication.

Recognize that your predecessors are symbols. A predecessor can be revered or reviled. One CEO will name the headquarters building after his forerunner. Another CEO won't wait a moment to denounce the incompetence of the jerk who came before him. Suddenly, you find old Higginbottom's portrait out of the boardroom and in the hall outside the loading dock.

Is it better to be kind or brutal toward a weak predecessor? There is no reason to honor a flawed leader, but there are not many grounds to actively defame him, unless such action serves a legitimate business purpose. Gorbachev may have had better reasons than most to defame a predecessor, but the accent should really be on the future. Be cautious. Many of the "antipast" recriminations I have witnessed in U.S. business are nothing more than spleen venting—energy directed toward a harmless scapegoat rather than a productive "villain." Managers should save their energy for the real villains.

Realize you are making history, not just following it. The manager must consciously consider the history he is making. He should glance at his actions periodically and see how they are coloring in the profile of himself. And he should consistently ask, Is this how I want to be remembered by my company or my department?

I think that David Rockefeller had an excellent grasp of this practice. After seeing Rockefeller on television talking about world economic matters, employees at the Chase would comment to me that they were proud to work at Chase Manhattan Bank.

Create symbolic value beyond your operational role. CEOs particularly should find ways to link with symbols beyond their specific jobs. For instance, Occidental Petroleum's CEO Armand Hammer is linked to the Soviet Union. Jay Pritzker, who heads up Hyatt, is linked with quality architecture. Dwayne Andreas of ADM, the grain giant, is associated with trade. Bill LeMothe of Kellogg is nearly synonymous with nutrition. Ford's Don Petersen is the quality guru. These issues are beyond performance. The manager must remember that his great performance successes of today will probably be forgotten tomorrow. The broader role will be remembered, if the manager makes the investment to develop it.

With most executives retiring in their sixties, symbolism must have staying power. Therefore, an association with a big issue like trade or foreign relations is a good anchor. It's a symbolic association which can endure and support your public profile for a long time.

Break with the past creatively. With Henry Ford as president, the auto giant Ford tangled with Walter Reuther and the fledgling United Auto Workers Union in the renowned "Battle of the Overpass." This legendary confrontation pitted security people from Ford's Service Department against the union organizers at Ford's River Rouge, Michigan, plant in 1937. Henry Ford II became Ford's president in 1945 and was also no sweetheart with the unions. In fact, as Leonard M. Apcar relates, the lunch-bucket crowd dubbed him Hank the Deuce. Still, he proved he could break with past tradition and was known to have ordered hot coffee sent out to striking workers picketing his Dearborn plant. Anton Dreesmann, the legendary Dutch retailer and one of the wealthiest men in Holland, has been a part-time professor of economics at the University of Amsterdam while building a $9 billion business. Both these executives knew the power of challenging tradition. (They also knew executives don't have to be aloof and contemptuous of the assembly-line worker or the college student.)

Observe how others study management symbolism. The symbolism of corporations is actively read inside and outside the company. We all know the squabbles that arise when managers of equal rank occupy offices of very different sizes or with different views of the outside world. The higher up you go, the worse it gets. Not only are you watching but the whole world seems to be watching.

In analyzing the relative power of the chairman and the CEO at Texaco, the *Wall Street Journal* saw a shift: "In the 1986 annual report, Mr. Kinnear's picture was bigger than Mr. De Crane's. In the 1987 annual report, their pictures are the same size."

Any citizen, and particularly any shareholder, should ask himself a perfectly intelligent question: What in the world do these considerations have to do with running a business? Nonetheless, managers scaling the rungs of corporate influence must be concerned about these symbols because that's how the world reads corporations. Nine months after the *Wall Street Journal*'s Texaco piece, *Fortune* published a feature article questioning if Jim Kinnear or investor Carl Icahn was in charge of Texaco. It kept the speculation alive that Texaco had not been successful in putting the leadership question to bed. (This speculation is ridiculous. Kinnear and De Crane are world-class leaders in a $35 billion company that, by its record, has demonstrated it artfully deploys its executive talent.)

Some people say, "Do your job and the rest will take care

of itself." I say, "Do your job, and spend your spare moments thinking about your 'positioning,' and how you are building your influence, because no one else will."

Do the organization's work. I have had the good fortune to counsel Monsanto's CEO Dick Mahoney over the years. When Monsanto was in the process of converting itself from a standard-issue chemical company to a diversified business reliant on the most advanced technology, a significant change in mind-set needed to take place. As Dick Mahoney explained, "The organization had to explore processes in biotechnology where we might not know the answers for ten years. I didn't feel that I could really understand what the people on the leading edge of our company were doing unless I experienced it myself. So, I spent one day a week for the next several weeks in the laboratory learning what we were doing and how it was done."

The great thing about this example was not just the symbolic behavior and the message that it sent to the organization but it's also saying that management has a duty to learn about the behavior that it expects from the company's employees, what their behavior entails, and how it works.

Dip down into the organization as a creative force. Jack Welch of General Electric is a manager who really knows how to teach by example. He participates in the creative planning sessions, but not constantly. He knows that if he's there all the time, he'll shut down the natural dynamics. People will be trying to please him. But, he must show that he is willing to do "shirt-sleeve thinking," that he can contribute in a free interchange. GE's continuing record of innovation shows it is a creative company.

Take ceremonies seriously. Too many managers scoff at such things as twenty-fifth-anniversary cakes and retirement dinners. You don't have to go to all these events, but when you do you make the honored guests feel as if they are being acknowledged for something important. Remember your high school graduation or your bar mitzvah? Which people do you have the warmest memories of? Weren't they the ones who made you proud of your achievement?

Beware of the trappings of power. Power trappings have become dangerous symbols because they suggest power abuse. One of the first things to happen after a hostile takeover or a leveraged buyout is that the corporate jets go on the auctioneer's block. It's like dismantling the king's coach, a symbolic attack on power trappings.

One of the epic cases of abusing the corporate trappings was unveiled in 1986 at Allegheny International, the owner of Wilkinson Sword and Sunbeam and Oster appliances. The August 11, 1986, issue of *Business Week* chronicled a steady fall in profits since 1981 with a loss in 1985 of $109 million on $2.1 billion in sales, and mentioned the company's purchase of a Florida condominium in which Allegheny's Chairman Robert Buckley and other top AI executives owned units. The article went on to list other unusual perks for a company deep in the red: "At one Florida [management] gathering, an ice carving [gracing] the banquet [table costing] about $10,000 according to one key former executive," an elaborate wine cellar ... installed in [the CEO's] home by an AI subsidiary ... three former executives [saying] the company paid bills for the purchase or shipment of wine* for this cellar. A total of $32.3 million in executive loans—some used to aid executives in stock acquisitions, others for other purposes—and a fleet of five corporate jets dubbed the Allegheny Air Force."

---

*In the article, *Business Week* didn't clearly establish if the company had or had not been reimbursed for the wine.

Business Week later reported that one week after the *Business Week* story broke, the CEO stepped down. With such revelations, is it any wonder that Boone Pickens and Carl Icahn have had a field day portraying American business as the refuge of feudal lords exploiting company assets?

Assess the risks of being an eccentric or a maverick. To gain and hold influence, a manager must do some things that are carefully calculated. Occasionally, brilliant maneuvers are required. Others are "no-brainers." A surprising number of managers run aground because they overlook the obvious. Managing obvious symbolism is a matter of vigilance not brilliance. Some people run their lives or their careers with a devil-may-care attitude. Being careless or eccentric has its price. I'll never forget this nugget I read in the *Harvard Business Review:* "Some companies may say that they like wild ducks, but only if they all fly in the same direction."

Not all of us have the cunning or the cash of a Howard Hughes who can get away with doing the outlandish. Everything you do to put yourself outside of the mold has its price. The price may be that you are regarded as so irresponsible or reckless that no one will dare rely on you and have his own image jeopardized by being associated with you. Companies do want imagination and creativity, but they will tolerate only certain sorts of maverick behavior and it better be related to what they perceive as their needs at the time.

Respect the power structure's appetite for the symbols of order. Remember when auto executive John DeLorean left General Motors in 1973? DeLorean, who ran GM's North American car and truck business, had made public questions about his future at GM. He said when he resigned, "I have to do [things] in the social area, and, unfortunately, the nature of our business just didn't permit me to do as much as I wanted." A week after he resigned, DeLorean was appointed to head the National Alliance of Businessmen. Who was the chairman of the NAB that picked DeLorean? Dick Gerstenberg—who was also chairman of General Motors. GM needed to put a good face on DeLorean's departure, and I suspect that the one-year stint at the NAB was tied to DeLorean's severance arrangement with GM. The automaker simply couldn't afford to have a wild duck flying out of its top management without things looking carefully orchestrated.

DeLorean's case was highly visible. It showed that the power structure has a distinct preference for order. Influence and power work according to certain rules. You have to know the rulebook to play the game.

Strive to be a symbol for the organization. One of the best ways to stand out in any organization is to understand its values and then show how you embody them. You don't have to be the CEO to be a symbol. And the CEO, if he is worth his salt, is delighted to showcase other symbolic leaders within the company.

Look at the annual report, the CEO's speeches, the press releases. What does this company want to get across about itself? What qualities are praised? Are they risk-taking skills, innovativeness, reliability, ingenuity, bottom-line focus, strategic insight, technical excellence? Usually it's four or five traits. See which ones are part of your makeup, and then exploit them. Constantly review the work that you and your people do and point out the fresh, innovative ways you are breaking ground using values your company esteems. If your company gives high marks for risk-taking skill, and that's something you're good at, regularly point to the risks you've successfully taken. Do so in an understated but clear way. Your goal is not to boast or gloat. It is to give your boss or bosses the information, so they can point to you as a symbol for the organization.

Find the right times to demonstrate courage and then stand up and be counted. There are moments when you have to show the people around you that there is a right thing to do and it must be done. This goes beyond being a symbol for the organization. It is quite simply having and showing integrity. When Jackie Robinson put on a Brooklyn Dodger uniform in 1947, he became the first black baseball player in the major leagues. At opening day at Ebetts Field in Flatbush, you could hear people booing in the stands. PeeWee Reese, the Dodger shortstop from Louisville, ran to Robinson and stood next to him. Eventually, the entire Brooklyn Dodger team strode to Robinson and stood by him. In minutes, the cheers and applause drowned out the boos. That was a memorable example of taking a positive stand.

Time and again, I have turned away lucrative business because it represents a conflict of interest. I often remember the phrase that Hill and Knowlton's Chairman Dick Cheney taught us: "We stick with the girl we brought to the dance." In the short run, it loses business. In the long run, it earns respect, the best clients, and great fees.

A manager who fails to take a stand at a critical time will also be remembered ... and none too kindly. He will be known as *the man who was not there.*

11

How to Read the *Wall Street Journal* in Three Minutes

Part Five concerns how you can deal with the media. Yet I also want you to look at the press as a consumer, that is, a reader. In order to increase your influence as a manager, what should you be reading, and *how* should you be reading it?

Consume the "power" columns and journals. Many managers ask me what the top business leaders read. The *Wall Street Journal*'s "Economic Report," which appears on the front page each Monday, is a "must" overview of the current business climate. Joel Kurtzman's articles, which appear in the Sunday *New York Times* are always filled with insight, as are Steve Shepard's *Business Week* editorials, and Marty Barron's column in the *Los Angeles Times*. The *Nihon Keizai Shimbun* from Japan and the *Financial Times* from London can be found almost everywhere in the "civilized" world, and I would recommend you try to read them at least three or four times a month. You should also flip through Morgan Stanley's monthly research reports. They give you a great feel for business trends. Dean Rotbart's publication, a newsletter called *TJFR* (*The Journalist and Financial Reporting*), should be mandatory reading for every CEO and public affairs head in the United States. Skimming it, you will quickly get a feel for the agenda of the press, its hot buttons, and its new directions.

Focus on the key writers, not the publications. There are probably three publications in the United States where pound-for-pound, every day, the reporter may understand your industry as well as you do: the *New York Times*, the *Wall Street Journal*, and the *Los Angeles Times*. They have the budgets to carry the best staffs. Often the reporters have more competitive information than your entire research department. You will find great writers in magazines and in papers like the *Washington Post*, which concentrates on politics, but usually not as many as in the three dailies just mentioned.

It's the reporter, not the masthead, that matters. Many think that reporters read the *New York Times* to find out what is going on. That's not true. Instead, they read individual writers on the *Times* staff. They follow the writer not the publication. It's important to know the power journalists, especially if one of them covers your industry. When I worked closely with individual reporters, I got to know some of these people very well. The late Everett Clark of *Newsweek* knew more about space than any other writer alive and more than most space officials, too. Roger Benedict from the *Wall Street Journal* really understood the oil and gas industry. Stuart Pinkerton, when he was at the *Wall Street Journal*, was a great aviation expert. Dick Witkin, the aviation reporter at the *New York Times*, was in the same class. Writers of this caliber were regarded by all others in their profession as *the source*. Likewise, there are security analysts who are comparably authoritative. They are the ones who are quoted most often in the best stories.

Read the *Wall Street Journal* in three minutes. I hear many managers complain that they simply can't stay on top of their business reading. Yet, I see so many businesspeople on airplanes and in airports who don't know how to read the business press. They don't practice aggressive reading. It's clear that these people are pressed for time, and yet they read a business publication just as if they were reading a novel.

It's a rare morning when my reading of the *Wall Street Journal* takes more than six or seven minutes. If I'm pressed for time, I can easily get what I need in three minutes. Granted, I don't read every feature, but I get the essentials. Speed reading has almost nothing to do with it. It's a question of dismantling the paper into its most vital parts and consuming those first.

The number-one thing to do is to scan the "Who's News" column and find out who has lost his job or moved up a notch. The next thing is to go to the front page and run your forefinger down column two. Those will be all the significant business stories for the day. Check if your industry or your company is affected. Then look at the headlines of the three *Wall Street Journal* lead stories on the front page. Next, go inside to the first pages of the second and third sections respectively. The top center or right is normally where the major trend stories are. For the third section, that story will be about a major trend in finance. There, you take in the headline at least. If you have any time left, turn to the editorial page. You look at the last paragraph in each editorial which essentially sums up the *Journal*'s position.

It may shock advertisers, but you've just read the paper. The *Journal* has long touted page three as its best ad space because that's where the lead story of the day is continued. Frankly, unless they're involved in that story, the real opinion leaders stop reading it on the first page. I've always felt that the page to advertise to reach opinion leaders is the "Who's News" page. My approach to the *Journal* is similar to the way that Henry Kissinger absorbed TV news when he was national security advisor and then secretary of state. Kissinger has been quoted in *Impact: How the Press Affects Federal Policymaking* as saying that he never watched the evening news: "I was only interested in what they covered, and for what length of time, to learn what the country was getting."

Learn from the "fringe elements." A fair number of managers today grew up in the radical times of the sixties and seventies. I'm sure many read and still remember I. F. Stone's weekly, *Mother Jones*, or the *Village Voice*. Once these rebels checked into Wall Street, some stopped renewing their subscriptions. That's too bad, because there are some valuable lessons to learn from the radical and alternative press.

I expect that we will witness a resurgence of radicalism in the 1990s—not sixties' style to be sure, but radicalism nonetheless. Because of television and the acceleration of communication, I also expect that radical ideas will move into the mainstream far more quickly than they once did. Business generally studies small business to learn innovation. It tries to re-create the "skunk works" ingenuity of businesses operating from garages and basements. Likewise, society's thought leaders still study the radical pockets of thought in our culture to look for innovation.

Most of us have a hard enough time reading the *Wall Street Journal*. How does one begin to keep track of the radical and alternative press? I have found one way that's not just instructive but fun.

There is a bimonthly publication from Minneapolis called the *Utne Reader*. The *New York Times* has described it as "the Swiss Army knife of New Age counterculture for people too busy to read magazines" and the "distant early warning of the far-out." Editor Eric Utne picks his shots from publications as far-ranging as the *Chico News & Review*, *Ms.*, and the *Ecology Center Newsletter*. Utne's articles declare "The Dawning Age of Sloth," talk about activism in Eastern Europe, and introduce entrepreneurs as "the real cultural revolutionaries." Why should businesspeople bother about the alternative press? Because the alternative press—and the people it serves—have an interest in business as a way to achieve their objectives. A recent issue of the *Reader* proclaimed on its cover: "If Marx and Jesus were alive today, each would have an MBA." That's a drumbeat I wouldn't ignore.

The Japanese think that spiritual values are coming back and will be a big thing in the nineties. You see that trend in these publications. You also hear about the resurgence of old-fashioned romanticism. Today's global executive must have a constantly updated understanding of rapidly changing values.

Part III

INFLUENCING THE MARKETPLACE

12

Intelligence Gathering

Frederick the Great said he could excuse being defeated but never being surprised. I know plenty of executives who feel that way, too. Today, any executive's power triangle must be supported by first-tier intelligence.

It was the fall of 1982, and Wall Street was awash with rumors that Allied Signal and Martin Marietta were cooking up a deal to prevent Bill Agee of Bendix Corporation from taking over Martin Marietta. Unfortunately for Bill Agee, his intelligence-gathering capability was not up to par, and he chose to ignore the rumors. Had he been on top of things, he would have investigated, verified, and mounted a counteroffensive.

If Coke's CEOs had better intelligence, they would know why Pepsi beats them so regularly and relentlessly in supermarket sales. Pepsi is constantly studying consumption patterns, retail distribution channels, promotion schedules, and a host of other factors, and this gives them a leg up.

Mike Miles, the new CEO of Kraft General Foods, is the sharpest marketer of American consumer goods. The powerhouse behind the growth of Kentucky Fried Chicken, he's now doing the same thing at Kraft General Foods. Why does he win? Because he has a voracious appetite for intelligence, and he's very much aware of the other side's intelligence-gathering efforts. He's so careful that he has his company's travel people glue stickers on airline ticket jackets cautioning his executives not to talk shop while en route!

While it is true that intelligence gathering in the business world is not quite the equivalent of the military's cloak-and-dagger stuff, the military is a role model for the business world. In fact, I wasn't surprised to learn that Parker Gilbert, chairman of Morgan Stanley, after graduating from Yale spent three years in army intelligence.

Here are a few simple rules:

Learn how to combine information. One of the toughest tasks in intelligence is ferreting out an accurate "translation" of seemingly contradictory information. George Taylor of Jane's Information Group (which publishes the renowned *Jane's Fighting Ships*) told me, "In a recent analysis we did of a $15 million acquisition, we had five authoritative sources. Three appeared to hold one position, and two nearly the opposite. The typical management reaction is simply to accept that as two opposing viewpoints. We make strong efforts to reconcile contradictions. It took the efforts of one of our very best analysts to add the data up properly and find the single consistent message that unified all the input and resolved the contradictions. When we did, we knew the acquisition was a smart one."

Similarly, there is a lot of seemingly contradictory information about the buying behavior of consumers. Consumers want gourmet taste and few calories. They want freshness and long shelf life. They have equally strong drives toward bargains and quality. Marketers need much more exact intelligence on what consumers really want. This need is forcing a change in how consumer data are being collected. Instead of looking for snippets of data about loosely defined consumer groups, today's research centers on tightly defined segments. It even looks at the behavior patterns of individuals in great detail. This latter technique, called single-source research, may monitor a given individual's viewing habits, shopping behavior (through item-identified grocery receipts), and subscriptions and direct mailings. The seeming contradictions start to break down once the study target is more sharply defined.

Never underestimate the usefulness of public data. Managers are constantly dismissing publicly available data because they are not exclusive. This is foolish. If you want to understand your competitor's problems, look at the analyst reports from the brokerage houses. The largest financial firms publish more than 1,800 reports each year. Another source is public-record discovery in court cases. Discovery exposes enormous amounts of information. Your competitor is usually not anxious to see this data published, and the value can often be substantial.

Jane's relies very heavily on public data, and George Taylor says that public data are extremely rich sources of information for the defense industry. If that's the case in the tight-lipped province of national security, imagine how much public data may be available in your industry! For example, if you want to know what cereals General Mills is bringing out in a year, monitor the Trademark office every few months. Trademarks are usually registered one to two years in advance. If a trademark is registered for a cereal called "Choculas," it doesn't take a genius to figure out that a chocolate-flavored cereal shaped like little Draculas is on the mind of General Mills.

Make your facts persuasive. In 1941, an enlisted man practicing on the Pearl Harbor radar was told to ignore the flock of planes that crossed his screen. In 1978, no U.S. bank would have believed that a decade later eight of the ten largest banks in the world would be Japanese even though that trend was well underway then. Sometimes, new information is too far afield from what management accepts as plausible no matter how *real* it is. The true master of business intelligence helps people to accept a wrenching new look at the world. He helps people understand how the seemingly incredible could be true, and why it's essential to act *now*.

Study what you're already paying for. I am shocked at the number of executives who don't digest a clutch of research studies every couple of weeks or once a month. These things are readily available. Most company libraries or research departments subscribe to them. It takes only ten minutes to read through the executive summary. These reports tell you what's happening, what's on people's minds, but many managers just don't take the time to learn.

Learn to sift the data efficiently. We are conditioned to think that unless information is current and self-evident, it's probably not important. That attitude costs us dearly as global competitors. Some vital intelligence may *seem* hopelessly outdated, but it is actually very relevant; some is buried in minutiae.

Cargill, the largest private company in the world, is a major force in commodities trading. In excess of 50,000 messages a day flow between their headquarters outside of Minneapolis and the trading desks and outposts in the fifty countries where they do business. Each of those messages may contain 800 to 1,000 characters, and it's not unusual for a commodities trader to receive 400 to 500 such messages each day. What will the messages be about? Rainfall. The Kansas wheat crop. If rain isn't falling, the alternative crops the farmers will be planting. How weather or political conditions on one side of the globe affect prices and demand on the other. All of these data are being churned through the twists of a twenty-four-hour market.

Successful organizations today must know how to absorb vast amounts of information and act on it quickly. The *shoga shosha*, Japan's big trading companies, such as Mitsubishi, and their Korean counterparts, the *chaebol*, such as Daewoo, are the most impressive networks of worldwide information gatherers since the Fuggers launched the idea of a business newsletter in 1609. The Fuggers were a German merchant family whose success as traders was largely built on their ability to gather and use information to their commercial advantage, which involved information such as the impending fall of a royal house, the expected quality of the wheat harvest, or breakthroughs in making glass or smelting metals.

Today, the Japanese are Fuggers on a grand scale, endlessly collecting and sifting through apparently meaningless details for the essence of trends. I will go into meetings with Japanese businessmen to be astonished at what they know. They will not only have totally up-to-date information on my business, but they will also have read and dissected speeches that I gave ten years earlier. They understand how my thinking has changed and what forces were most influential in molding it. They also see my blind spots.

As business globalizes and competition becomes more complex, we will need to gather more data. Increasingly, it's easier to find the data than to find the time to digest them. Indeed, the problem with intelligence, too often, is not the lack of information but the abundance of it, a situation that drives some managers to throw up their hands, reject exhaustive research on principle, and operate on gut feel. Nothing is more dangerous. The trick is finding and using high-capacity minds who can digest huge amounts of data and come up with the essential kernels. Intelligence pros will tell you that sifting out the important from the unimportant is the most essential skill they look for in an intelligence officer.

Pass intelligence through a sieve. As intelligence data move up the management ladder, they should be more "focused." Each succeeding management layer should shape the data and winnow them, without destroying the vitality or urgency of what is left. Ultimately, the data that reach the top should concentrate on the key points of the CEO's agenda.

Monitor worldwide. This advice may sound extravagant, but it's indispensable. The *Asian Wall Street Journal*, the *Financial Times*, or *Die Neue Zürcher Zeitung* will often carry stories that signal competitive moves. An inexpensively retained European academic, or even a graduate student, who scans the business press abroad can become a cost-effective field agent.

In most of Western Europe today, it's possible to watch yesterday's evening news from the States early the next morning. How many U.S. businesses think of monitoring the newscasts in Brussels or London? If you are an Ohio firm that makes high-voltage ceramic light fixtures, and your most important competitor is in Singapore, you'd better be monitoring the Singapore press and financial marketplace for news about the firm's breakthroughs and plans.

Study your competitors' published statements, house organs, public reports, speeches, and ads. You always have to look around the corner to see what your competitors are doing. Some companies carry the attitude that "There's no need to know my competitors. I have my own agenda, and I'm just going to follow it." This attitude assumes that your adversaries' agendas don't have an impact on yours, and that's dangerous. Earlier, I suggested looked for public data on your competitors that they didn't go out of their way to publicize. It's also important to look at what your competitors or adversaries do to publicize themselves.

It's amazing how transparent most businesses are. They have to be. You can't tell your outside public one thing and your own people another, and not expect to confuse your employees. It's hard for any sizable business to operate under camouflage, and you can use this to your advantage.

Study your competitors' ads and announcement calendars to learn their sense of timing. How long before bringing out a product do they announce it? What season of the year do they usually make their organizational or product announcements? Almost all organizations build their public momentum (and to a large extent, their internal momentum) off of their marketing calendars. Look at a company's total public output for a given year—their ad campaigns, trade show approaches, product launches—and you will often detect some important nuances about how that firm chooses to compete.

Make everyone an agent. Train everyone in your organization to gather data. First, it gives employees at all levels a healthy outward focus. Second, it compels your managers to weed out important from unimportant data as it progresses up the management ladder. Third, you will be surprised at how much data worth verifying come from unexpected sources, such as a casual comment at the grocery store. The first lesson that employees of the Japanese and Korean trading companies learn is to be ever watchful for information that could help the firm.

Always protect informers. Not all intelligence gathering is external. Within organizations, you will find people with different motives coming forward to give you inside data. The most important rule regarding inside intelligence is to shield the sources, because the risk in coming forward may be substantial. The data may be valid or off the wall, but the source should always be given sanctuary. Otherwise, you may turn off the spigot. Some informers don't intend to be informers, so it's especially important to learn what you can from a variety of sources, such as job candidates from competing companies who interview with you. I'm not talking about trade secrets, but valuable information concerning culture and attitude.

Emphasize analysis over espionage. The weight in all kinds of intelligence activities has moved from espionage to analysis. Former top national security sleuth Herbert Meyer in his book *Real-World Intelligence* (Weidenfeld, 1987) observes, "Today in virtually all of the world's best intelligence services, the heavy action has shifted from the operational side of the house to the analytic side." It's equally true in business. Some of the best executives I know come out of the research departments of ad agencies, where their job is to analyze mounds of data.

Establish the real size of the battlefield. Intelligence is the only way to determine the size of the influence problem you are trying to solve. If managers would do some sensible snooping before they tried to exert influence, they could often save themselves a pile of grief and money. Von Clausewitz, the great military strategist, once wrote that the enemy always looks bigger and more ominous in the heat of battle.

Create listening posts. We have offices in Adelaide, Australia; Hilo, Hawaii; and Ankara, Turkey. Our people in these places gather data in different time zones and monitor the "tone" of news coverage and reaction. We also have a critical office in Auckland, New Zealand. Why is it important? Because Auckland is the first place you can trade stock on any given business day. In a volatile takeover contest, it can set the kickoff value and the day's trading range.

Conceal what you know. Of course, individuals and businesses must obey the disclosure laws, especially in financial transactions. Still, many arbitragers trade on intelligence, and shield their maneuvers legally. Since the 5 percent ownership level of a company is the SEC-mandated disclosure point, many arbs will hold stock at just below 4.9 percent. They are not yet compelled to show their hands so they don't run the stock value up.

Make policy analysis a management duty and perhaps a full-time position. You must gather intelligence on all the forces that could trip you up, not just on what your competitors are doing. Is a cutting-edge state about to pass bellwether legislation that will reduce the water capacity of toilet-bowl tanks? Why should you care? Well, it could require your company to redesign its entire line of plumbing fixtures. Is the Commerce Department going to shift import policy on canned tuna? If you're in the grocery business, a raised tariff could mean you'd better find a different tuna supplier.

Many companies still think too narrowly about intelligence: They think it's important to marketing but to little else in the business. A few companies, especially utilities, such as Arizona Public Service, have created policy analysis positions. When the policy analysis post is working as designed, it will identify significant trends early and propose intelligent responses. Without a doubt, the most successful policy analysis chief is Pat Choate at TRW. He has had a clear effect on shaping economic and educational policy in this country. His prominence as an author and speaker has also helped transform TRW's image from that of a manufacturing to a technology company.

A couple of years ago, an astute policy analyst in a beer company would have spotted the emerging power of MADD (Mothers Against Drunk Driving) and suggested building messages of moderation into beer promotions. Some of the leading breweries have now taken exactly that stand. A policy analyst, monitoring FCC deliberations, could have anticipated liberalized censorship standards for broadcast materials and revised the scripts of a major studio that went into costly production and then had to be altered.

Trade associations can conduct policy analysis for you. In large companies, however, much of it must be done in-house. A director of policy analysis examines input from sources as diffuse as the energy specs for new appliances to the English literacy level of the average new employee. The result is a constant flow of potentially useful suggestions that make a real difference to the influence a business has over its audiences and its destiny.

Use "soft soundings" to gather personalized intelligence. At Hill and Knowlton, we often use a relatively inexpensive means of gathering intelligence for our clients. Soft soundings are not "projectable" in a strict statistical sense. Therefore, I class them as intelligence rather than survey research. They can still give you a good feel of how a company or a person is regarded. In influence strategies, that can be critical information.

Let's say that a technology company is about to make a public offering of its stock. Three days before the offering is to be floated, a spate of reports emerges from customers that the firm's new disk drive system has been breaking down at an unexpectedly high rate. Should the firm delay plans for the offering because the negative news will drive down the value of the stock? Or should it go ahead with the offering because its otherwise strong reputation for quality and customer service will make the problem unimportant? In such a situation, it would be very difficult to conduct a systematic opinion survey. The opinion leaders are a very small group. The time frame is short, and the issues are quite technical.

Confronted with a problem of this sort, the first thing I would do would be to create a "blind," that is, conceal the identity of my client, which means identifying two or three other computer hardware firms in roughly the same product area. Then, I would jot down a list of eight to ten people who are regarded as authorities on this industry. The list would probably include a couple of security analysts, bankers who invest heavily in this sector, several large users of such equipment, a respected trade journalist, and perhaps a retired manager or two from the industry. I would then devise a list of questions to ask these people, for example, "How do these three firms compare on their reputation for quality?" "Do any of these firms have a reputation for conspicuously good or bad quality?" "How trustworthy and reliable would you say these different management teams are?"

Sometimes it's not necessary to shield the company's identity, but usually it is. In this case, it would be essential. I would then call my contacts and note down their remarks. What they say to me is not attributed to them under any circumstances; if it were, most people wouldn't talk freely. Since I have proven myself as a trusted confidant, and since I'm "neutral," they feel comfortable being candid. Their help to me is a chit drawn on the Favor Bank. Using these data, I can then consolidate the opinions and advise the company if it should proceed with the offering.

Become an intelligence source for others. The senior editor of one of America's leading women's magazines retains us to monitor the breaking news that comes off the wire services. When we read on Reuters and UPI that Nancy Reagan had breast cancer, we instantly offered this editor to national news desks as a credible spokesperson on the emotional impact of breast cancer. Her publication has studied the issue countless times. Journalists—print and broadcast—want that kind of input as the story breaks, not in a stale follow-up a day later. The exposure extends the influence of the editor and her publication, and the authoritative information the public gets is obviously valuable.

Often important financial news will be released after the market closes in New York, which makes it too late for most eastern and many midwestern news editors. However, I know economists and security analysts in New York who have built reputations for themselves and their firms in the Midwest and on the West Coast because they have specialized in being available for press calls on breaking news *after* the market closes.

Competition to be a recognized spokesperson is keen and the benefits are many. The best know that you have to keep your ear to the ground constantly and react very quickly if you are to be the source cited.

13

Research– Debriefing the Marketplace

In winning the U.S. presidency in 1988, George Bush used an integrated marketing strategy that pinpointed voters so successfully that while he won only 54 percent of the popular vote, he won an overwhelming 79 percent of the electoral vote. Like Reagan before him, Bush used a very carefully devised—and smart—strategy.

How did Bush and Reagan do it? First, they made a very careful sampling of which issues were important to a broad cross-section of various demographic groups across the country. From it, they learned that issues such as the economy, taxes, education, and crime were at the top of the list. Then they sought ways to associate themselves credibly with solutions to those problems. Next, they constructed persuasive messages on the issues they had identified.

On a recent shuttle flight between New York and Washington, D.C., Jim Granger, now president of the Wirthlin Group, gave me a particularly lucid account of how Ronald Reagan had won the presidency in 1980: "When the campaign began, it looked like Reagan had a substantial ideological gap between the average voter and himself." On the other side of the ledger, while Democrats had 51 percent of the voters' allegiance, in the spring of 1980—compared with 28 percent for the Republicans—the Democratic coalition that elected Jimmy Carter in 1976 had begun to fray. Rather than focusing just on the mainstream Republican vote, Reagan scanned the vote market to see what groups he could weld together to win the Presidency.

To take advantage of the breakdown in the Democratic forces and to create a mass that could carry the election, Reagan's people focused on several key groups: "The somewhat less-affluent and less-educated voters, union members, blue-collar and middle-aged voters. Through the use of extensive research, Reagan's people saw that these segments of the population, superficially at odds on many issues, nonetheless often overlapped in holding one or more of three major value outlooks on life: traditional ethics; belief in a strong leader; and a 'can-do, America!' attitude.

"Traditionalism, leadership, and strong optimism were naturals for Reagan," said Jim, "and created the glue that bonded a winning coalition."

Now that communicators have learned how to use research to shape and influence campaigns, they are revolutionizing marketing, lobbying, and every other form of influence that relies on public support. These techniques were first applied during the presidential campaign of 1980. The architect of the strategy was Dr. Richard Wirthlin. Hill and Knowlton has had a strategic partnership with the Wirthlin Group for several years now, and we have been the first to apply the principles learned in these campaigns to business situations.

The use of modern research began with marketing, but now it extends to every aspect of business. Today no intelligent firm would decide to build a plant that created Title III hazardous wastes without surveying the public attitude toward such a facility very carefully. Nor would a firm build a distribution center that would significantly increase truck traffic and noise before it understood a community's stance toward congestion and noise abatement.

Before, companies would just jam their decisions through, believing that their economic power in the nation or in a region would justify anything they chose to do. Now they recognize how indispensable research is to maintaining their real influence. You, too, must learn how to use research.

Use opinion surveying to shape your influence strategy. The computer has made us razor-sharp in defining and reaching market segments. Point-of-sale and zip-code analysis allow striking new approaches to get to the people you must influence. Mass audiences don't make the decisions in our society anymore. Rather, a series of opinion cells have to be addressed one-by-one and often molded into a coalition. Through opinion surveying, you set up a dialogue with representatives of the needed cells or niches. We have the information technology today to do that, and successful firms are learning that they must do it.

Target your messages to constituents who matter. In 1988, the Bush campaign matched its messages to the characteristics of key voting blocs. The Republicans, for example, would certainly win if they won the South. The Democrats could only win if they won the South. For the Republicans, the South was an opportunity; for the Democrats, it was a survival issue. Portraying the Democrats as big-spending, soft-on-crime "liberals" was a simple and effective message. It went a long way toward undermining southern confidence in the Democrats. In the West, Bush's themes were more upbeat; in the Midwest, they were more focused on jobs. Group by group—ideologically, geographically, economically—the Republicans crafted the consensus they needed to win the election. They looked at the range of acceptable beliefs they could embrace to create the consensus, and they engineered the outcome. The Republicans were no more manipulative or malevolent than the Democrats. The Democrats tried to do the same kind of thing. They were just far less effective at it.

Build nine-digit zip codes into your marketing strategy. Imagine that the United States is a huge board of electrically illuminated "cells" that turn on and off to respond "yes" or "no" to any given attitude or viewpoint. That's how a sophisticated modern researcher looks at the United States. In fact, the nine-digit zip code allows us to divide the United States into nearly ten million residential "blocks." In much of the United States today—and soon in all of it—phone surveyors and other researchers will be able to pinpoint attitudes and outlooks with amazing accuracy. The implications stretch far beyond elections. Such data already govern what items are carried in a particular chain's supermarket and which are not carried in the same chain's store just two blocks away. The data determine which households get targeted mailings on a school bond issue and which do not. The data decide which advertising circulars are stuffed in your Sunday paper and which aren't.

Master the power of geodemography. One of Hill and Knowlton's sister companies in the WPP Group is Reese Communications. Reese, a highly specialized communications strategy firm focusing on direct-mail and direct-telephone approaches, is a master practitioner of geodemographics, the next step beyond demography. Lynn Pounian, president of Reese, has orchestrated some remarkably effective campaigns employing geodemographic data, that is, the use of census data on where people choose to live (or are forced to live) to predict how they will vote, what they will buy, and how they will look at issues.

When AT&T was directed to divest its regionally affiliated Baby Bells several years ago, it risked losing the fees it charges for access into the system that AT&T had built. AT&T gave Reese a "mission impossible": Find a large segment of the population that would support paying a higher phone bill to fairly compensate AT&T. By busting up the nation's population into clusters, Reese succeeded in identifying 1.2 million people who actually wrote their senators to raise their phone bills. It was all a question of correlating characteristics, values, and geography so that a targeted direct-action campaign could be waged.

Reese's cluster segments for the United States are a colorful array. The pie is cut in about twelve slices. For example, there are the "Technocratic Elite" where three out of every ten people are millionaires. There is the "Brunch Bunch," the group that has deep concern about choosing the *right* brand and getting good service. Another patch on the population quilt is occupied by the "Mad-as-Hell Blues." These are the blue-collar workers who sport NRA bumper stickers, hate any large business institution, the Ayatollah, and City Hall. The tactic for a large company wanting to be chosen by this last segment: Make your competitors even more hated than you are.

Avoid the risks of policy without polling. Not everyone believes in polls. Nor can everyone afford them. Jesse Jackson used no polls in the 1988 campaign for the Democratic presidential nomination. I'm sure cost was an issue. Instead of polls, Jackson relied on a steady stream of people giving him advice. On the plus side, Jackson was able to read the emotional tone of the people better than his opponents. His messages had a certain directness and clarity. They didn't sound as though they were homogenized to satisfy many different groups. It also worked against Jackson. His opponents placed infiltrators around him who succeeded in planting a fair number of wrongheaded ideas. These made Jackson sound inconsistent at times.

In the summer of 1988, I visited with Reverend Jackson in his hotel room, and tried to tell him where his campaign was misstepping. He asked me what the most important word was in the English language. Remembering his speeches, I said he must think it to be *perseverance*. He said no, that it was *love*. I looked at him squarely and said that in his case it was *trust*. A large segment of the population didn't trust him. That's what the polls were saying. Jesse Jackson listened and made some adjustments in his campaign.

Screen the surveyors. I learned the importance of this from our Decima research operation in Canada. When they do political polling, they are very careful not to have strong partisans of any political belief on the phone asking the questions. The general public knows enough about polling today to start rigging the results when they are hired as phone interviewers. A surveyor with a personal agenda of any sort is just like a computer virus. Both destroy the integrity of information.

Use focus groups to debrief customers. The focus group is the most efficient way to debrief customers or potential customers. The focus group is also an admission that the researcher doesn't know the "simple" questions needed to get the "simple" answers that are tallied up when you do conventional research.

What makes the focus group different from the traditional opinion survey or straw poll? The focus group brings together people—usually ten to fifteen—often with similar economic or social backgrounds. They talk about an idea or an issue, trying to bring it into focus. Unlike most opinion surveys, the answers are open-ended; the judgments are qualitative. The goal is not to come up with a projectable outcome; rather, it is to learn the motivations behind the answers. Still, while the people's viewpoints are individual, who they are as individuals is not an important factor, as it is in the "soft soundings." They are simply representatives of a group.

The moderator, who must be carefully trained to facilitate but not direct the outcome of the discussion, is critical to the success of any focus group. Often the moderator comes from the same socioeconomic background as the focus group and knows how to ask questions in a way that isn't manipulative or threatening. Sometimes management representatives look on during these two- to three-hour sessions through one-way mirrors. Participants are told in advance that their behavior is being observed and that their comments are being recorded. The identity of the company conducting the focus group is almost never revealed and is usually masked by mentioning it only along with its competitors. The participants may be paid $30 to $250 for their time.

As instructive as focus groups may be in getting insight into a market, managers have to know how to use this kind of output carefully. Since focus groups are still relatively new on the scene, general managers who use them, especially for the first time, will do well to keep some guidelines in mind. You should expect anyone who will manage a focus group for you to have these basics down cold.

Make sure that the focus group represents a clear market segment. Mexican Hispanics in Texas hold quite different views from Cuban Hispanics in Florida. Puerto Rican Hispanics are just as different from Mexican-Americans in California. Sixties' Democrats don't have the same outlook as New Deal Democrats, and both groups are quite different from the Democratic-voting "partisan poor," as Norman Ornstein, Andrew Kohut, and Larry McCarthy point out. When someone promises that they are going to create a focus group of Hispanics or Democrats, seniors or schoolteachers, find out *exactly* what they are talking about. Ask them how they are going to guarantee the integrity of the sample group, which is important to you.

Demand unvarnished input. Reporting unvarnished input is one of the hardest communications skills. Insist that the material reported to your management group includes the exact words and images used by the participants. Nothing undermines the purpose of a focus group more than a "smart" interpreter who tries to reduce the findings to his own summary view of the world.

Videotape focus group meetings. Management needs to see the intensity and the interpersonal dynamics that accompany the responses. By the turn of the century, almost everyone in management will be a product of television. You can wave reams of quality-control reports and customer-complaint letters at your lab chemists, and they won't register. But, if an unrehearsed group of consumers says your lemon-scented car polish smells like bad cheese, you have probably found a way to get through.

Make sure you're making sense to your customers. When using focus groups to get consumer opinion on potential new products or concepts, always make sure these are described in terms of existing products and concepts. Many firms make grave errors presenting new products to customers in too abstract a fashion. Think through the concepts visually and consider using models, charts, videotapes, and other visuals to explain the idea.

———

Testing is another aspect of research that can help build influence.

Test your appeal angle. You should never pay to place a story, because you can never control what you are going to get. However, you *can* test certain story angles and have a pretty good idea how they will be covered. Some hucksters sell their services based on their ability to place a story in a particular publication. A cover story in *Time* might cost $25,000; front page, right column of the *Wall Street Journal* might be $22,000; Sunday business page above the fold in the *New York Times* might be $19,000. These arrangements are called paid placements. I think that the idea of paid placements is preposterous, a little like the old practice of selling religious indulgences. The agent pockets the money, and the client never knows what juicy piece of gossip or bad news was used to get the story written.

I oppose paid placements. However, it *is* possible to test where a story is likely to end up being covered, and that's essential to influence. I support story testing as a modern and effective influence strategy.

In any national campaign, it's almost always possible to test how a certain story angle will play. We may take an idea with three different angles to three demographically similar California cities like Bakersfield, Stockton, and Fresno. We'll then look at the publicity generated. Unless it's an extraordinarily heavy news day, the results are usually very uniform. Some ad pros will doubtless retort that when you buy ad space or time, you can be sure it's there, but today's powerful TV zappers can wipe out the most beautifully constructed broadcast commercial. Your message is far likelier to reach the consumer if it is placed in the program content or the news material, and that is the goal of strategic marketing.

We handled publicity for the Harlem Globetrotters tours for years. We managed it like a science. The Globetrotters used to present an average of 289 events a year. So we tested, systematically, the results we got from various story angles and media approaches. We knew exactly which story would play best six weeks before the event, which played best forty-eight hours before, and which was best done at half-time (Globetrotter travel trips, the basketball clinic at the local elementary school, the mayor presenting Meadowlark Lemon with the key to the city).

Angle-testing technology is in its infancy. Here's a technique we are testing right now. An executive will give a speech or a public affairs program will be shown before a test-sample audience of fifty or sixty people. Each audience member will have an electronic flicker, a little like a TV remote control. They are asked to register positive and negative reactions at any point while the speech or program is in progress. The time of each impulse is recorded and corresponds to exactly one point in the spoken text or program. You can compare the reactions of an audience of high-tech workers in Albuquerque with those of senior citizens in New Jersey. You can get a pretty good idea of specifically what sells and what doesn't. There are any number of measurement tools like this one being developed right now.

14

The Need for
Bad Guys—and
Good Guys

When Marathon Oil defended itself against the takeover attempt of Mobil (a fight that I will discuss in detail in Part Four) great care was taken to photograph the monolithic Mobil Oil headquarters at 150 East 42nd Street. Panning from the ground up, we showed it as austere and threatening. Here was Darth Vader and the Evil Empire all rolled into one.

By contrast, we presented the Findlay, Ohio, headquarters of Marathon as the epitome of Norman Rockwell country. Of course, both companies were multibillion-dollar enterprises, but Marathon (with our help) took advantage of the fact that its headquarters wasn't a stainless steel skyscraper looming over Grand Central Station. Seeing the two sites made it easy to imagine that the giant vampire from the East would come into verdant Ohio and suck up the very lifeblood of the company, the town, and the people.

Mikhail Gorbachev has done a spectacular job of dramatizing the villains facing Soviet society, villains as disparate as overconsumption of vodka, former Premier Brezhnev, and meatless dinner tables. He's attacked indifference and the suppression of free speech. Most important, Gorbachev has known how to dramatize his wars for the benefit of the rest of the world.

Gorbachev has a host of skills when it comes to the care and feeding—and exploitation—of villains. He knows how to get the press and other onlookers to judge the legitimacy of his actions, and thus give them the feeling that they are, somehow, participating in his historic reforms. He does this by making his villains *universal* villains.

What follows are some of the ways in which you can use a villain or two to your, and your company's, advantage. And by the way, if you need any more good examples, just remember what George Bush's handlers did with one Willie Horton.

Don't think all villains are ogres. Some of the most fearsome villains are destructive, even though well-meaning. These are the "soft villains." They want employee entitlements, safety features, and product assurances that would send the cost of doing business, and the cost of the products, sky-high. Small businesses, for example, have been the center of job growth in the United States in recent years, but bills to increase the minimum wage and to expand their health insurance obligations could undermine the economics of small firms.

It's best to attack soft villains for the consequences of what they want, not the individuals or the demands themselves. This approach doesn't mean that smart businesses will back away from attacking soft villains, just that they must redirect the attack to show the outcomes of do-goodism, rather than make an ad hominem attack on the personalities involved.

Throw your adversary into disarray. Your appeals are most effective when they cause the opposition to "fragment" in defending themselves against the attack. Bush did this very successfully when he attacked liberalism as "the L-Word." When hurling it at the Democrats as an accusation, *liberal* meant lots of things. What kind of liberalism should the Democrats defend and uphold? Should they defend liberalism at all? By the time the Democrats had re-formed ranks, it was too late. Bush had created the disarray that screamed weakness.

Wendy's, the fast-food chain, caused disarray when in 1984 it unleashed Clara Peller to holler "Where's the beef?" True, Wendy's hamburgers had more beef. Nobody doubted it. But, the chain took a simple, passive difference and turned it into an aggressive weapon. Wendy's competitors scattered and stumbled in their responses. In the meantime, Wendy's gained important ground.

Another way to throw adversaries into disarray is to take the uniqueness away from their messages. Levi invented life-style advertising for jeans. Now, a host of other jeans manufacturers make it nearly impossible to recognize which brand is doing the advertising. Duracell, for years, touted the superior staying power of its household batteries by showing competitor batteries dropping dead right and left. Duracell-powered toys triumphed in shootouts. Finally, Eveready started showing its own ads with super-battery-powered heroes. The net effect: Who knows today which message stands for the stronger battery?

Don't make an emotional appeal too brazen. In 1982, the natural gas contract for the city of San Antonio came under fire. There were real concerns about sources of supply, potential shortages, and pricing. At the time, we were working on behalf of Valero, a billion-dollar company and the largest natural-gas-gathering company in the country. It had originally been a spinoff of Coastal States called Lo-vaca, but we helped change the name in Houston to Valero. We helped decide to move it out of Houston to San Antonio to get it away from Coastal States and to give it a softer image. (At the time, Houston had a brassy, big-money tone to it—a city that seemed dominated by the international energy conglomerates.) We also helped Valero create a board of community leaders, not just top businessmen, intending to give it more of a San Antonio twist and a more cosmopolitan base.

At that time, Valero had to raise prices to buy gas in the tightening market. Liz Carpenter, Lady Bird Johnson's former chief aide, joined me in San Antonio to organize support for the price increase. We tried to point out how real the probability of shortages was. The then-mayor of San Antonio, Henry Cisneros, saw political opportunity in fighting Valero's position. Cisneros was the budding Hispanic politician of the day. He believed he had widespread emotional support, but he miscalculated its depth.

On Christmas day, he secured time from the local TV stations to deliver a half-hour message on the gas issue. He branded Liz and myself as outsiders who were brought into town in order to twist the minds of San Antonians. He called us the two biggest propagandists in the country and said this was just a scheme on the part of the gas company to part the citizens from their hard-earned money. The plan backfired on Cisneros. The well-respected community leaders were outraged that the mayor had used Christmas day for his crass campaign. There were even some activists among the leaders. In essence, they said, "Henry, we need the gas. Enough is enough. For you to use Christmas day like this just isn't right."

Attack innuendo vigorously. Once, in Chicago, Hill and Knowlton competitors were "mongering" rumors that we were having tough times. The rumors were false, but the competitors were using the lies to fuel their recruiting efforts aimed at our people. We were staffed to the right level, but if we simply avoided the issue we would needlessly lose solid counselors. The solution was simple. We took out ads in the paper announcing an aggressive new recruiting program for ourselves that could only have been supported by a very healthy business. Our adversaries backed off, and we actually landed a few of their best people in our net.

Create your own vocabulary. Bush did it with "Read My Lips," "The Furlough," and "The L-Word." He persuaded many through his calls for a "kinder, gentler nation." Effective slogans and vocabulary are invariably short in length. They must play on the jargon of the day and be rich in emotion. Most successful appeals in our marketing-intensive world have a strong element of language innovation.

Don't paint yourself as a choirboy. Let them know you are a terror, but make sure they don't forget how much of a saint you can be, too. Peter Drucker has said that he learned more theology teaching management and as a management consultant than he ever did when he taught religion. "For management," Drucker says, "surely deals with the nature of man, the nature of God, and, alas, occasionally with the nature of the devil, too." Show that you have a rough-and-tumble side, especially if someone crosses your path.

Be feisty when you need to be, but also wrap your righteous anger in your good deeds. Both Dayton-Hudson in the Twin Cities and Arvin Industries in Columbus, Indiana, were able to use their outstanding records of corporate social responsibility to rally the public and state legislatures when necessary. The tactic helped defend both companies against hostile takeovers. In calculated defenses against raiders, these two firms were smart enough to be righteously indignant about the assault on them, and scrappy about every intrusion on their turf.

Sell the promise before the product whenever you can. Hardly any of us has seen high-definition television yet, but consumers surveyed are convinced it's better than regular television. The same is true for those mini-cassettes of digital audio tape that few of us have heard. Before they even tasted it, a number of journalists decided New Coke didn't taste as good as old Coke. New Coke had such a legacy to deal with that it was bound to fail. Anticipation is very important to the development of markets. Successful anticipation is built mostly by marketing communications and not by advertising strategies.

Anticipatory marketing is happening throughout the world today. Thus, firms like Sony were anxious to erect billboards for electronics items in Beijing. Few can afford fancy consumer electronics today, but tomorrow the opportunities could be vast.

Manage the grapevine. As Regis McKenna of Silicon Valley related to Tom Peters, a company "can even organize a 'word-of-mouth' campaign." Certain firms have tremendous potential to sway opinion by this means. These are the firms with great quality in a highly desirable market niche, and with a very soft-spoken public image. Because they overdeliver, they provide what marketing professor Phil Kotler of Northwestern University's Kellogg School calls the "delight factor," which people love to extol. At get-togethers and over lunch, cluing someone onto an "undiscovered" overdeliverer is one of the most treasured tips a person can bestow: "Have you tried? . . ." In the past, Apple Computers, Volvo, BMW, Reebok, and Dove Bars have all fit into this category, and some of them still do.

Never let your rival turn "news" into a competitive advantage. If you are going to lose a major customer, assume that your competitor will make headway out of it. Company A recently won a major service contract from General Electric. This is a large-volume account with a prestigious client. Initially, its rival, Company B, lost the contract. In fact, the account wasn't even profitable for Company B, and they suspected it wouldn't be profitable for Company A, either. It would be just a "prestige" victory for Company A. Rather than sit back, we counseled Company B to take the initiative and get the real story out to the industry and among analysts before Company A even released its "victory" announcement. The newsworthiness of Company B's disclosure got them instant coverage and gave their story valuable credibility. Company B regained control of the agenda.

Introduce friction. Make sure there's no peace. There are countless examples of small- and medium-size businesses that gain turf by causing friction. McDonald's and IBM are two examples of giants who continually stir up the pot. McDonald's is the top quick-service restaurant operator in the United States. Time and again, McDonald's innovates before the competition requires them to do so. In 1973, they came out with the Egg McMuffin and revolutionized American breakfast habits. In 1987, they recognized the trend toward lighter dining and introduced their fresh salad entrees, and in just two years these salads have catapulted to almost eight percent of McDonald's sales. McDonald's has a knack for staying ahead of the market. IBM does it the same way. In the last ten years, they have pioneered masterslice technology in building high-density circuits and innovated voice-recognition systems. Not only do IBM and McDonald's launch the innovations but they publicize their launches in a bold, snappy way. When I hear about an innovation from IBM, my reflex response is, "How do they keep on coming up with these great new ideas?" Great leadership firms make sure the market around them is restless.

One of our clients keeps what I call a full-time "press terrorist" on the payroll. His sole job is to undercut the authority of competitive claims. As in "Mission Impossible," management would disavow any knowledge of his activities, but he is very incisive and remarkably accurate in destroying the competition's arguments. He spends his time analyzing competitive claims and talking to the press (off the record) about what they should look for in critiquing competitors. He sustains perpetual friction in that industry. He wouldn't be successful unless he had tremendous credibility, so he never tries to whitewash his own brand or firm.

It's not a new idea. At Hill and Knowlton, I once worked with a man named Bill Depperman. He spent entire days writing letters to editors about ghoulish automobile crashes. Whenever there was a particularly horrifying auto crash, Depperman would research it. He would go to the site and photograph head-on collisions on undivided four-lane highways, and take pictures of cars and trailers that had careened off steep cliffs. He dramatized the events to demonstrate what could have been averted if a steel guardrail had been in place. Depperman's offensive moved plenty of local politicians to put up the guardrails you see today on dangerous curves. This crusade was not, however, a personal one. Bill sold a lot of steel for the members of the American Iron and Steel Institute. He also, I'm sure, saved many lives in the process.

Get authorities to endorse you. I'm not talking about Lorne Greene getting behind your dog food. That kind of endorsement doesn't cut it anymore. Advertisers are using more and more endorsement from actual authorities. What doctors say about pain relievers really does matter. So does what automotive surveyor J. D. Power says about cars. Because there is so much uncertainty in today's society, people crave the clear endorsement of some established specialist behind an idea or a product.

Mix your punches. Use an assortment of persuasive tactics. Some people may think that George Bush and Ronald Reagan were elected president because they had such awesome campaign war chests to pay for their advertising. In fact, their advertising was better focussed, but Bush and Reagan relied much less exclusively on advertising than did previous presidents.

The Bush victory in 1988, and the Reagan landslides in 1980 and 1984, were definitive proof of the power of marketing communications, and that means advertising plus. These wins showed that influence over the electorate could be exerted only by an integrated campaign: one that combined sophisticated public affairs and communications strategies with conventional advertising. *Focused Impact* is the name of the marketing strategy they used. It employs multiple channels—speeches, talk show appearances, releases, position papers, and advertising—to hammer home a limited number of key themes and raise them above the national message clutter.

Let's say the topic is education. First, Bush would give a speech on education. Then, the position paper on education would go to the press and the think tanks. Scholars friendly to the Republicans, congressmen, and cabinet members would reinforce the education theme in their own talks. Then, there would be an advertising blitz with an education slant. In a concentrated time frame, education would snowball to the very top of national consciousness. In the future, only such integrated marketing strategies as Focused Impact are likely to influence the public on big topics.

Emphasize execution over ingenuity. People often associate marketing with creativity, with creative genius. Creativity translates in our minds to a clever jingle, a stunning photo, or sizzling copy. All those factors may be important—they may even be necessary—but they will not, alone, win a marketing campaign. The central feature of successful marketing is disciplined execution. The message or the idea has to get to the customer in the planned way. The failure to get to the

125

customer is killing all that brilliant network advertising. It's also hurting many other ingenious marketing programs.

Not long ago, I learned about a recent promotional game. Played on a card where the customer scratched out the answers, this promotion was done by a leading fast-food chain. The results were far below expectations, so they investigated. The problem turned out to be quite simple. In the restaurants that had a lot of foot traffic, upwards of 1,400 customers a week weren't getting the game cards from the staff behind the counter. They never had a chance to play the game on which millions of advertising dollars were being spent. That's typical of how marketing programs fail today.

Today, promotions are complex, and will become more so. Thus, they won't work in businesses with anything less than first-class operating disciplines. Any marketing thrust must match the company's ability to deliver at a given point in time.

15

The Attack
Agenda

In 1985, when South Korea was planning for its
role as host of the 1988 Olympics, we were approached by SLOOC—the acronym for their Olympic committee. The first thing we told them was to
change their name; SLOOC sounded like a disease!

When South Korea first approached us, we
pointed out that people had a lot of questions about
Korea, questions about their political stability, their
attitudes toward the West, the attitudes of young
Koreans toward their own "establishment." Was the
Korean infrastructure going to be able to handle
things? Would the various athletic sites and the Olympic Village be ready? In other words, was Korea
ready for a challenge of this scale?

In our first meeting, I told the Koreans to put
together a fourteen- or fifteen-point program, a plan
that would bring the country together and make the
Olympics a decisive turning point in Korean history.
The first five of these objectives were to be relatively
easy to achieve, and I told the Koreans to celebrate
after achieving each one of them. But the Koreans
rejected the idea. In my opinion, had they followed
the plan they would have generated sufficient posi-

tive momentum. But they didn't, and the Olympics became a showcase for poor planning, missed milestones, and a considerable amount of divisiveness. The South Koreans used old-fashioned, out-of-date public relations strategies, and as a result they ended up with a terrible image in the West.

The advice we had given them boiled down to setting some easy initial goals and then declaring victory. That, and the other principal maxims of the attack agenda, are explained in the following pages.

Businesses that are leaders expect to be attacked. Most of the product innovation and even more of the job creation in the United States is coming from medium-size businesses. These smaller businesses—the Davids—don't have the market share yet, but they have the agility to win one-on-one. They have learned how to divide the market into ever-finer slices. Davids *can* slay Goliaths, and not just in marketing but in the public affairs area, in merger and acquisition battles, and in internal communications. The second-place business that doesn't attack will probably lose its ability to defend itself.

Attack is what any upstart must be prepared to do. But understand that if you are the upstart, the attack tactic may be suicidal if you haven't thought through your plan with great care. Several writers on business strategy (such as Ries and Trout) have applied these time-honored principles of warfare to business contests in general. It's my intention to look at them from a communications standpoint.

Attack the weakness in the leader's strength. Every strength creates its own weaknesses. A company that is big and dominant is most often slow and inflexible. An efficient manager is frequently cold and heartless. A compassionate organization is frequently undisciplined. Seek out the weaknesses in the leader's strength and exploit them. Assail them with relentless focus and intensity. Editorial writers long ago learned that these weaknesses make the best copy. Go for the less evident chinks in the leader's purported strengths.

Time and again what cripples the leaders in any industry or profession is the apathy that leadership brings with it. Is it any surprise that *Business Week* anointed not Harvard, not Stanford, but Northwestern as the number-one business school in the nation in 1988? The traditional leaders got sleepy. Northwestern saw that basic disciplines and a focus on marketing were going to be the essential management skills for the next generation of business leaders, and that's where they built their strengths.

Attack on the narrowest possible front. If your enemy's strengths are vast and its resultant credibility is high, pursue it in only a few selected areas. In the copier industry, Canon attacked Xerox on price and portability and won a major share position. Antiabortion forces achieved steady growth in support by focusing totally on "the right to life" and painting anything that infringes on that right as murder. Especially in communicating, the more areas you choose to attack, the more complex your message becomes and the less likely you are to register a strong impression.

Operate from the smallest defendable base, and praise the value of that niche. Häagen-Dazs, the runaway market leader in premium ice cream with $300 million in annual sales, is careful to keep its focus tight. Häagen-Dazs hasn't strayed into ice milk and low-calorie brand extensions. It took its share of the market away from larger ice-cream makers, and it's not trying to become the biggest itself.

Working out of smaller Midway airport, Midway Airlines captured valuable share on domestic routes from carriers like United. Midway's distinctive edge is convenience to the Chicago Loop. I doubt Midway will ever be as big as United, but it has a clear defendable niche.

In their communications, both Häagen-Dazs and Midway pound away at their key advantages. For Häagen-Dazs, it's premium quality. For Midway, it's convenience.

Outflank but do not provoke the leader. As you look for the leader's weaknesses, try not to raise alarm or suspicion. You gain nothing by making the leader attack you. Mark out positions that the leader will see as either irrelevant or foolish. Sorrell Ridge was a pioneer in the all-fruit segment of the jams and jellies market. This was back when all-fruit jams could be found only between the granola and the tofu in your local health-food store. Sorrell Ridge made a point of attacking the dominant Smucker's sweetened brand in head-to-head TV comparison ads as early as 1985. Sorrell Ridge continues to do very well, but they also roused Smucker's to respond. *Forbes* reports that Smucker's has retaliated with its own unsweetened "Simply Fruit" brand with sales that "are even slightly better than Sorrell Ridge's . . ." Sorrell Ridge may have gained important stature in attacking Smucker's, but it is now squarely up against Smucker's formidable marketing and distribution expertise.

Examine the business or the constituencies that the leader is walking away from. Gitano saw the jeans makers were walking away from the mass-market jeans business toward higher price points. Gitano, which studied the marketing expertise of Procter & Gamble, decided to create an "aspirational," trendy image in its marketing, but stock its products in the K Marts of the world. The result: outstanding business growth. Gitano sold the romance, but made it available to the masses.

Attack competitors' lines at their furthest point. The optimum situation is to pinpoint a competitor's division that is both important and weak and is, as well, a reasonable distance from the headquarters. In the days of von Clausewitz, to whom I owe this bit of advice, it was simple to say "longest point" and have it universally understood. Today, longest point should be taken to mean "most difficult to get to," with at least a couple of plane changes and no good hotel in town. Outdo your competitor in community giving there. Suddenly start courting the financial community in that city. Recruit a couple of good employees. Persuade the city to honor you as a favored corporate citizen. In short, you can find any number of thorns that will draw your opponent's attention to this remote location. Remember, the more inconvenient, the better.

Threaten your adversary at his home base. It may seem paradoxical, but it's equally effective to lob a "grenade" at your adversary's headquarters. It proves his mortality right in the place everyone expects him to be invincible. For this reason, a successful attack on your adversary's home base can really boost the spirits of your own organization. This is exactly how the people at Pepsi feel about the Pepsi Challenge taste-test campaign mounted in the Coke-dominated South. The Pepsi Challenge was more a morale issue than a sales issue. It gave Pepsi, the classic underdog in these areas, a rallying cry around which programs could be built. For Coke, it worked the other way: It seemed like an omen. If consumers preferred the taste of Pepsi to the taste of Coke, even in those areas that Coke dominated, what would the future bring?

Divert your adversaries by causing them to doubt the loyalty of *their* allies. I routinely make it a point of calling on the CEOs of my competitors' largest accounts with useful information. The visit takes me no more than thirty minutes; the recovery time for my competitor is generally two to three days.

Sabotage your competitor's timing. If you get wind that your rival will hold a gala press conference to bring out a product, preempt! Stage your own counterconference first. We recommend this tactic to clients who are in a race to bring a new product to market.

A competitor of a baking yeast maker was about to trumpet a new fast-rising yeast product. Learning of this, the second firm rapidly organized an event to unveil its new comparable product three days ahead of the competitor. The event celebrated the product and talked broadly about new opportunities. Through good distribution, graphics, and story design the national press appetite for stories about yeast was sated. When the competition's news conference rolled around, the press wasn't biting. As one reporter put it, "How many stories about a given category like raisins or car phones or frozen yogurt can you do in a month?"

Opportunistic companies will always look for ways to preempt their opponents' access to the media. Another way to sabotage your competitors' timing is through attacking industry conventions. I can remember when Montgomery Ward had a major turnaround in performance after years of serious losses. Retailers habitually release their preceding month's sales results on a particular day of the following month. Ward's then-CEO Steve Pistner and his people just decided to advance the calendar a day and release their sales early. Of course, the rest of the industry was incensed at this breach of etiquette, but Ward's got important attention . . . and how much do you value your competition's affection anyway, especially if you're the underdog?

Reward early defectors handsomely. Hire away talent from the leader. Consciously overpay for certain people you recruit, and thereby damage the leader's compensation picture. Of course, you have to make sure that you recruit real talent. Once you have done so, put these people on a visible, fast

track to prove that you offer greater career opportunity than the leader can. This action can have powerful symbolic value.

In 1983, Taiwan offered $2.5 million in gold to any mainland Chinese pilot from the People's Republic of China who would defect, and bring his MIG jet with him. In the end, the Taiwanese didn't win the political showdown with the PRC, but the technique was an imaginative one, and pilots actually did defect. Had the struggle gone on long enough, and had Taiwan collected a steady stream of defectors, the next step in the strategy would have been to lower the price, as tangible evidence that they were winning the war. Of course, the key here is publicizing what you are doing. The real benefit comes from the headlines.

Enlist collaborators behind enemy lines. The allies made heavy use of the French Resistance during World War II, not just for military purposes but for propaganda purposes as well. When Three-Mile Island became news, the anti–nuclear power movement was quick to enlist local residents who lived in Harrisburg and Middletown, Pennsylvania, as national spokespersons against nuclear power. It's important to have testimony from people who live under the leader's "tyranny." A twist on this is to encourage disreputable people to collaborate with your adversary. I once suggested to a client, only half-jokingly, that they hire Ivan Boesky to do testimonials for their chief rival.

Call up the militia. Arm the people. Whenever you can, get the public on your side and publicize it. This tactic is what made the Pepsi Challenge so effective. It recorded the conversion of religious Coke drinkers as they experienced the revelation of Pepsi. This tactic is what makes the statistical survey of new car buyers done by firms like J. D. Power so persuasive. As consumers become more sophisticated in using statistical data in selecting products, and

voters do the same in picking candidates, we will see more and more use of surveys. Surveys are the roll call of the marketing militia.

Attack whenever the leader fails at innovation. It's easy to embarrass a leader who can't stay abreast of innovations. Look how Pepsi killed Coke over New Coke. When the innovation flopped, Pepsi's ads trumpeted: "The other guy finally blinked." When Sears reverted to "everyday low pricing" by changing its pricing structure after decades, the competition had a field day. Customers were cool, and Sears enemies verbalized the doubts: "Does this mean that Sears everyday prices weren't really all that low for the last century?"

Set easy initial goals and then declare victory. This advice is another application of the tactics discussed in Part One. Henry Ford's Model T and Chrysler's K cars were not quality cars, but they allowed Henry Ford and Lee Iacocca, respectively, to enjoy the momentum of early victories. The Model T's competitor was not the Oldsmobile or the Packard, but the streetcar. Ford put the car within reach of the average working man. Seen against the total spectrum of available cars, the K car was no great shakes, but it was so significantly better than the Chrysler products immediately before it that people took notice. Both Ford and Chrysler publicized how their respective improvements were turning heads.

You must, however, carefully avoid premature celebration of the goals you set. After a couple of quarters of performance improvement at Eastern Airlines, Frank Borman announced Eastern had achieved a "dramatic turnaround." Several months later Borman had to concede that Eastern was in worse shape than it had been in before.

Attack where least expected. When you're on the offensive, von Clausewitz says, be quick and overpowering. He also says

that the backbone of surprise is fusing speed with secrecy. That's the principle behind the Blitzkrieg. The key is not so much the speed but the timing. Identify every kind of "expectation" you can use against the leader. If he expects you to rush to the marketplace, you stall. If he expects you to advertise heavily, you use word-of-mouth. If he expects you to campaign in D.C., you lobby the statehouses. If he expects you to zero in on opinion leaders, you organize grass-roots support.

Obviously, good intelligence on what the enemy really expects is essential for this tactic to succeed. A good many dead generals have launched surprise attacks into the open jaws of a waiting enemy.

Let yourself be portrayed as lazy and unthreatening before launching a major offensive. But follow up that offensive doggedly. Siemens was seen as a stodgy, slow-paced electronics firm before an explosion of acquisition of activity beginning in mid-1988 and stretching into 1989 when it bought a majority interest in the Bendix automotive electronics group, acquired ROLM's manufacturing component from IBM and also created a ROLM joint venture with IBM for marketing and services, and waged a successful takeover of Plessey with British General Electric.

———

Once you start the campaign, don't let your rhythm falter. Von Clausewitz believed dogged pursuit was essential. For him, it stood second only to victory itself in waging war. An elegant first offensive that is not backed by heavy artillery and a complete campaign is a major error. It's a veritable invitation to a Balaklava.

16

The Defense Agenda

If you're on the top and get attacked, you should understand that's part of the privilege of being on top. You should not take it personally. You're guaranteed a lot of criticism if you are on top. Some of our clients cannot understand why people would want to criticize them for being number one. They instruct us to "Go out there and tell people all the facts! Tell them the way it is!" We have to explain that the reason they are number one is that they are good, but being good also gives the others a license to attack.

Everyone wants to knock off the Oakland A's, Notre Dame, and the United States. There's a big difference between being number one and being *secure* about being number one.

Surveys have shown that the leading brands of decades ago remain so today. Kleenex, Bayer, and Kodak are indestructible titans. It pays to lead. More sharply defined market niches and a whole new cast of global competitors are making it tougher to defend leading brand positions, but it's also more *valuable* to defend them.

Even when the brand is a leader in a seemingly "dying" category, companies will invest handsomely to defend their positions. The *Wall Street Journal* tells of Kraft's Cheez Whiz, the popular cracker spread of the sixties, which seemed fated for the culinary cemetery. It was the leading brand of cheese spread, but what did that mean in the trendy world of Camembert triangles and chunks of Port du Salut? Still, Kraft would not let go. It revived the brand as the leading microwave cheese sauce! In the same story we also hear that the British Beecham Group Plc. (now part of SmithKline Beecham) has kept Aqua Velva after-shave afloat, despite Pierre Cardin and Geoffrey Beene, reconcocting the fragrance with a more contemporary aroma.

The message is clear: The advantages of leadership are tough to replace. If you have them, defend them. But, how exactly do you defend your influence and leadership in a world that has devised so many new and ingenious ways to attack the top dog? Here are some tips on defense, civil and uncivil:

Never acknowledge an upstart by name. In the 1988 campaign, George Bush was careful never to refer to Mike Dukakis as anything more than "the governor from Massachusetts." When you give an opponent a name, you acknowledge that he is something more than a box on a chart or a title in a directory. Keep the opposition anonymous. As the leader, you are not compelled to recognize your betters, because, in the world of marketing ideas and brands, you don't have betters. Watch the consumer product advertising on television: It's always the number-two and number-three brands who call out their competitors' names. The number-one brand has no need to do so. Why should it give number two free advertising?

Be ambiguous about who number two really is. Why should you tell them? When you are the leader of a field with several weighty contenders, don't give your closest rival the distinction of being a clear number two. Always depict the rival as one of several who just can't do the job.

Never let your rivals change the rules on you. For years, AT&T had made available its UNIX operating system to a wide array of universities and computer firms. UNIX had earned a well-respected position as quite possibly the best global computer operating system to work across different brands of hardware. AT&T was not itself, however, perceived to be a threat as a hardware manufacturer. AT&T then surprised the international computer industry and announced it would proceed with the development of a new version of UNIX in collaboration with the rapidly growing California work-station firm Sun.

When this dispute began, UNIX was used predominantly in universities. Because it works on all different computing systems, it was seen as a business solution with widespread commercial impact. Competitors such as IBM, Digital Equipment, Siemens, Apollo, Groupe Bull, Nixdorf, Philips, and Hewlett-Packard were fearful that the new AT&T/Sun coalition could give AT&T and Sun an edge, if they controlled the development of a new version of UNIX. So, these eight competing firms grouped together to form a new organization, called the Open Software Foundation, to sponsor development of their own version of UNIX. The OSF response was rapid and decisive. It emphasized that the new UNIX system should help all competitors equally rather than giving a potential edge to any individual firm.

Use the high ground. If you're the leader, then you are king of the mountain. That doesn't just mean you should defend the high ground; it means you must use the high ground to your advantage. Never surrender the superior vantage point that being number one provides. IBM has always used its superior position to study how the customer is changing, and to respond to those changes.

On the other hand, Sears, which as the largest retailer in the nation has a better view of the customer than any other retailer, failed to see that customer preference was moving from house-brand to name-brand products. It didn't use its advantage to observe and to act quickly enough. Having a fortress on the summit does very little for you unless you use the lookout to study the terrain.

Know when to call for fire on your own position. That's a lesson learned by platoon commanders in the Vietnam rice paddies. Sometimes, you must attack yourself to save yourself. After the product-tampering episodes, Johnson & Johnson knew and communicated that it had to redesign its Tylenol brand. It withdrew the popular capsule and replaced it with a caplet, far more effective in foiling would-be tamperers. What would have happened had J&J not changed? Can you imagine the suggestive ads and press releases from competitors for the pain relievers "your family knows can't be tampered with"?

One of the greatest corporate transitions in modern times—and a successful one, too—was AT&T's evolution from the nation's largest protected utility to being another blue-chip competitor in telecommunications and technology. Suddenly, AT&T had to become a marketing company. I will never forget the speech then AT&T Chairman Charlie Brown gave to the Commercial Club of Chicago back in 1978 on the occasion of that redirection. He said, with the glow of a man who knew he was talking deep strategy: ". . . there's a new telephone company in town. . . . 'Ma Bell' is a symbol of the past . . . I would appreciate you passing the word that Mother doesn't live here anymore."

Both Johnson & Johnson and AT&T refused to be done in by disastrous blows. Rather than let the competition do it, they took the toughest steps against themselves first. Rather than being embarrassed about having to change, they communicated their changes clearly and with determination.

Make your adversary spend massively for share. It is always easier to defend than to attack. Burger King has exhausted itself time and again attempting to assail McDonald's. Ultimately, it cost Pillsbury (Burger King's one-time U.S. parent) the farm when it was taken over by British Grand Metropolitan.

Mock your opponent's boldness. I am indebted to B. E. Bidwell, chairman of Chrysler's Chrysler Motors subsidiary, for this story: Henry Kaiser had stoked away a huge fortune building ships, but after World War II he decided to get into the automobile business in Detroit. After all, with just three competitors—Ford, GM, and Chrysler—wasn't it time to extend the competition in the U.S. auto industry? Kaiser was better capitalized than another Motor City maverick, Preston Tucker. At a post–World War II Detroit press conference, Kaiser said that he was prepared to invest up to $100 million to go against the Big Three and establish a position in the automobile market. In 1946, that sum was roughly equivalent to $5 billion today. When the then-chairman of General Motors heard Kaiser's pledge, he hooted back, "Give the man one chip!" Even back in 1946, it cost massive sums to build market share.

Train enemy fire on decoys. Does your chief competitor believe you are going to start making home swimming pools in the next two years? Publicize that it's a possibility, but that you "don't know if the market will be there in the next five years." Plastics are not where your firm is headed in its diversification, but you can certainly say "they are an exciting area" at your next press conference. The important thing to remember is that your competition is likely to be listening to everything you say. The more decoys with which you can present them, without obscuring your own strategic course, the better.

When traditional marketing tools are neutralized, consider the "big event." PepsiCo is one of the sharpest marketers around. Besides its position in the beverage business, it is a dominant force in the fast-food industry with Pizza Hut, Taco Bell, and Kentucky Fried Chicken. PepsiCo's marketing world is a glimpse into what marketing will be like for many firms in the future.

Pepsi and Coke are entrenched combatants engaged in a war of attrition for millishares. (A millishare is a tenth of a market share percentage point, a thousandth of the whole.) In a $40 billion soft drink market, millishares mean big bucks. Both Pepsi and Coke are large, with sizable resources, and solid management. The bottom line in this duel is that the traditional marketing tools are neutralized. Both firms are going to put out fine advertising, but it's Pepsi's view that the advertising has to hook up to a bigger idea.

Joe McCann is senior vice-president of the corporate parent PepsiCo. As Pepsi's top communications expert, McCann has an excellent vantage point from which to look at Pepsi's marketing programs as instruments of communication and influence. "We are committed to the news event as a market-ing tool," he says. "When it works, it *really* works." Pepsi, for example, developed a promotion around the release of the movie *E.T.* in home video format. *E.T.* is one of the most popular films ever made, and Pepsi offered an enticing re-bate on the cassette as part of a promotion. When Pepsi treated the event as a news story, so did the press. "The result was big exposure for us," McCann says. "It was worth millions of dollars. But, for our kind of product, the news has to be pretty big. As far as we're concerned, tra-ditional marketing publicity, a talk-show publicity tour, for example, rarely has enough impact to affect big, older, established brands. The shortcoming of traditional market-ing PR is that while it makes a splash and delivers some 'reach,' it rarely provides enough frequency." It isn't re-peated enough or broadly disseminated enough to have the needed impact.

Use controversy intelligently. Pepsi tries, McCann says, "to create genuinely newsworthy events, usually something very new, very unusual, or with a touch of controversy. Our payment of $5 million to Michael Jackson in 1987 is a great example. It was risky and controversial, but we gained that money back in news exposure before the commercial ever hit the air."

As exciting as this approach is, it's not for the faint-hearted. Remember when Pepsi used pop-music star Madonna in an ad that mixed sensuality and religious symbols? McCann told me, "It's obviously not something we would want to repeat. But we learn from mistakes, both ours and other's, and move on fast to something new. Usually you can be more controversial than you might think, but you *can* go too far."

The lesson of big-event marketing is clear: You can't violate things people hold sacred, but you can certainly be more controversial in other ways and gain rather than lose. Sometimes the controversy is unintentional, as when Michael Jackson's hair caught fire during the filming of a Pepsi ad; sometimes the event can be linked to world affairs as when former PepsiCo Chairman Don Kendall served Nikita Khrushchev his first Pepsi in Moscow; or when Kentucky Fried Chicken opened its biggest restaurant ever on Tiananmen Square in Beijing.

The reason why Joe McCann's analysis is probably right is that our society is so much more pluralistic, and, if not necessarily more tolerant, we are all a good deal more curious these days. The public accepts things today that they would have rejected a decade ago, but they still have some key values that can't be violated without enormous backlash.

If you want your ideas to have influence, make them a part of the story line. Managers these days must think about exactly what will get the product in front of the consumer. From its inception, I handled the marketing and publicity for

Gatorade, the soft drink that replaces body fluids lost in active sports. The key for Gatorade was to get brand recognition from sports-minded people. How should we do it? Advertise on TV during sporting events? You know what sports viewers do at commercial time during a football game. They head for the kitchen to get a beer or a snack. The agenda we created for Gatorade was to make Gatorade a part of the game itself.

European sports-marketing firms like Adidas have long given publicity to sporting equipment brands through very visible markings on the uniform. They draw the product's identity into the game. A soccer player or a race-car driver in Europe looks like he's suited up in a sandwich board! In the States, that doesn't work. How about ads on signs posted around the stadium? Perhaps. But, wouldn't it be even better if we could still find a way to make Gatorade an active part of the game? If you want amateur athletes to buy Gatorade because it rehydrates you, show Heisman Trophy winners chugging it down when they have just finished an eighty-yard dash to the end zone. So, on the sidelines, we put huge chests of Gatorade with the trademark on the chest and added stacks of Gatorade cups.

As television added more sideline reaction shots and personal coverage of the players, televised football, to name just one sport, became a continuous promotion for Gatorade. It was the teams themselves that launched the ritual of dousing winning coaches with Gatorade or ice water from the Gatorade chests. After all, if these guys were going to get christened, why shouldn't it be from a Gatorade chest rather than a French champagne bottle?

The same principle is being used by countless manufacturers in getting their products in the movies. This works, of course, as long as the movie isn't just an excuse to trot out an endless stream of consumer products in cameo roles. Companies want a high-impact association. The *Wall Street Journal* says Glenmore Distilleries shelled out more than $50,000 to place a bottle of its Mr. Boston black raspberry schnapps on rock singer Joan Jett's dressing table in a key scene of the movie *Light of Day.*

Create ties to the gatekeepers. We promoted Gatorade in a number of ways. For example, we did cartoons for trainers. We knew that athletic trainers were an important audience for us to reach. They would have a say about what would be served on the sidelines. We studied the trainers and learned that most of them operated in barren, cinder-block offices that smelled of sweat and athlete's-foot powder. I remember taking a train from southern Connecticut one Thursday morning. I spotted a couple of renowned cartoonists who were bringing their weekly strips into Manhattan. It occurred to me that we could use the cartoonists to reach the train-ers. We set up a competition among some of the best of them. The cartoons wove Gatorade into the story lines. We printed the drawings and sent them to trainers all over the country. We mounted the pictures with a special adhesive on the back so the trainers could easily put them on their walls. We gave the trainers instant decoration for their offices.

Always check out a celebrity endorser (long before you go on national television). In 1972 and 1973, Gatorade sponsored the indoor tennis circuit, which covered a series of "second-ary" towns such as Memphis, Tennessee, and Salisbury, Mary-land. Television was the key to the whole event. Week after week, public television carried the circuit and relayed it by satellite around the world. We used this to Gatorade's advan-tage. I believe we were the first to position product signing so that the camera angle was "blocked." You couldn't possibly take a close-up shot of the tennis player without the Gatorade logo being the dominant image in the background.

We had tapped Ilie Nastase, the great Romanian tennis player (and alleged KGB colonel), to appear on the "Today" show. Nastase's booking agent was also alleged to be a KGB operative, whose chief job was to make sure Nastase didn't defect. His name was Ian Tiriac. Tiriac told us the star would be outstanding on the show and that he would hype Gatorade. I met with Nastase and Tiriac at the Brasserie, an all-night restaurant on 53rd Street. We sat down to have eggs and to talk about the "Today" show, which would be airing in an hour and a half. After twenty minutes, I noted Nastase hadn't said anything, so I turned and asked him, "What's the problem?" Tiriac jumped in, and said, "You should know Nastase doesn't speak English." We put Nastase on the show, but all he could do was smile and make gestures. I remember the look on Barbara Walters' face, which seemed to say: "Don't ever let this happen to me again."

Since then I have never trusted an agent's "tout" about how good his "property's" communications skills are. Now I check them out long before the property makes an appearance on television.

Look for ways to be part of a rivalry. I'll never forget the playoff game that pitted the Minnesota Vikings against the Los Angeles Rams. It was December 28, 1972, in the old, cold, open-air stadium in Bloomington, Minnesota. We had devised a scheme for the Rams to use hot Gatorade (because they're from a warm climate). Hot Gatorade would warm their veins and make their hands more supple. The Vikings made a real show of their toughness. At that time, Bud Grant forbade bench heaters because he felt they symbolized weakness.

The night before the game, there was a press conference. We positioned a question with Mike Rathet, the AP reporter, who asked, "Coach Grant, what do you think about this controversy of hot Gatorade versus cold Gatorade?" Grant responded, "Gatorade, hot or cold, we'll beat 'em either way." The press corps picked it up and gave the line terrific play.

At the game, I was on the sidelines with a couple of my associates. We kept going between the Viking and the Ram sidelines ladling up Gatorade. (Frankly, I spent a lot more time on the Ram side because they had the heaters.) I was supervising the serving of hot Gatorade. The Rams took an early lead. One of the big Ram guards, Tom Mack from Michigan, came over and told me what a terrific thing this hot Gatorade was. As luck would have it, in the fourth quarter, Joe Kapp threw a long pass to an end named Henderson who caught it for a touchdown to beat the Rams. The Rams were really angry. They chased me and my associates into the stands, blaming hot Gatorade for their misfortune! But, the rivalry was pure gold for the client.

Associate your product with cutting-edge culture. A Broadway play can end up as a real profit bonanza, but most plays start out simply trying to defray costs. There are agents on Broadway who will get your product written into the script of a Broadway play. I remember going to the producers of the revolutionary musical *Hair*. We said we wanted to get Gatorade into *Hair*. They said, "Great, let's hold a Gatorade party after the Wednesday matinee. We'll invite everybody up for a celebration onto the stage." You'll remember that *Hair* was a flower-child musical that ended with the cast and audience having a "love-in" on the stage. As the play closed, the cast said to the audience: "Please come onto the stage and share Gatorade with us." Again, Gatorade got terrific mileage from the promotion. The product was linked with a new, "in" movement, and it became a regular happening at the Wednesday matinee. We found additional ways to use it, such as publicizing the *Hair*/Gatorade association worldwide.

Look for ways to exploit climate, geography, and special events. We also developed the "Story of Thirst." We found a home economist by the name of Barbara Coad and put her on the road. She went to radio stations, TV stations, and newspapers throughout the South during the hot summer months talking about what caused thirst. We also worked with the legendary Olympic swimming coach "Doc" Council-man from Indiana University, and with Cynthia Potter, the Olympic diver. Doc would swim the English Channel, his body covered with oil to keep in the body heat. When he reached shore in Dover, he would take a swig of Gatorade. We worked with Jock Sempel, the trainer for the Boston Marathon. He agreed to have Gatorade served to the run-ners during the race in the ubiquitous Gatorade cups. It was the first time that this kind of thing was done. We loved it. And, more to the point, so did the Gatorade people.

Part IV

IN TIMES OF CRISIS

17

Marathon
Repels Mobil

.

On November 3, 1981, my wife and I had taken a client couple to a Notre Dame football game at South Bend. The mood was upbeat, as it always is when the Fighting Irish win. That stadium, perhaps because it gives spectators such a feeling of closeness to the field, compresses and amplifies emotions. It's impossible not to share in the euphoria of a Notre Dame victory—unless you traveled there expressly to root for the other side, a sometimes dangerous proposition. Fortunately, we had been rooting for Notre Dame.

We decided to tool the stretch limo to an unlikely dinner spot. Phil Smidt's is a legendary haunt in Hammond, Indiana, where they serve terrific fresh fish. Smidt's sits in the shadow of the Lever Bros. plant at the end of a rail spur on the backwaters of Lake Michigan. From the outside, it may look like a small, dimly lit, roadside inn, but Smidt's is both spacious and always packed. On a Saturday night, it's also energized, and this Saturday night was no exception.

Judy Ryan, my secretary in the Chicago office, had good powers of deduction. She knew that if Notre Dame won she could probably track us down at one of three places between Bloomington and the Loop. Phil Smidt's was number one. About 6:30 in the evening, I saw this burly fellow, drying his hands in a white apron, hobbling around the restaurant.

Over the din, I ciphered that he was paging "Mista Dilen-schneidah." Something was up.

Reluctantly, I left the table and got to the phone at the bar; the voice at the other end was Mike Rousseau, the vice-president of public affairs for Marathon Oil. He asked if I could get on a corporate jet Marathon was sending for me that evening, and be in Findlay, Ohio, late that night or early the next morning. Hill and Knowlton had been Marathon's PR counsel for twenty years, and of course I said yes. Then Mike went on to explain that Marathon had received an unsolicited takeover offer from Mobil Oil in New York and that Marathon was going to mount a takeover defense. Knowing this might well be my last night out for months to come, I went back and had a stiff martini.

With a couple of my associates, I got on the Marathon jet the next morning. We flew to Findlay, the Marathon headquarters, where we had lunch with all the officers at about 11:30. Marathon's CEO Harold Hoopman had wisely decided to draw all the officers and outside consultants together for lunch before we fixed our individual battle plans. I say "wisely," because too many CEOs bring in teams of different specialized consultants and then keep them separate. The result is that each of the specialist teams competes in designing the general strategy, the specialists are underutilized, and valuable time and energy are lost. In a well-managed strategy, the specialists feel free to consult with each other—as they must—while everyone knows his specific role.

The others in the room included Bruce Wasserstein, then the leading mergers-and-acquisitions ace at First Boston (he is now principal of Wasserstein, Perella), and Dick Pogue of Jones, Day, Reavis & Pogue, Cleveland's leading law firm. At the end of lunch, Hoopman stood up and addressed us in an impassioned way; he thanked all the consultants for coming, and all the managers for being there. His remarks showed great dedication.

You have to be very careful in situations such as this, and Hoopman was. Marathon didn't yet know the full dimensions of the Mobil offer, and in that posture the law expressly prohibits management from protecting a company from takeover, unless the values offered are clearly below what the shareholder receives if the firm remains unacquired.

We then grouped into specialist teams to talk about immediate tactics, and came together later in the afternoon with Dick Pogue to discuss the initial public communications. It was already clear that we would fight Mobil on a public affairs front as well as on a financial and legal front. Mobil had a troubled public reputation, and that weakness looked like their Achilles' heel. In fact, public relations might be the cornerstone of the Marathon defense, but we needed to do some planning first. What we needed most was time.

In the meeting, Dick said he would be going to Columbus, Ohio, in the next few hours to try to talk with federal judge Joseph Kineary there about getting us more time. In fact, Dick didn't go to the judge in Columbus. Instead, he succeeded in getting a temporary restraining order from a Cleveland judge. Did I feel betrayed by him? Well, I felt surprised, certainly. I later confronted him. "Dick, how could you do this and not tell me?" His response was, "How could I *not* do it? I had to do it in order to make sure we had the time we needed to do the things we said had to be done." He was concerned about potential leaks. Tactically, he was right.

Another momentous event happened later that Sunday afternoon in the Marathon boardroom when Bruce Wasserstein gave Hoopman the contract for the First Boston fees. Wasserstein handed Hoopman a file folder with a document to sign. Nothing was said, but you could tell by the way that Wasserstein looked at Hoopman that Wasserstein was saying, "Sign this or we won't represent you." It was a bill for a $1.8 million retainer, which in those days was big money. It was nothing compared to the $20 million attorneys' fees for three weeks of work that Marty Lipton and Wachtell, Lipton, Rosen & Katz got for defending Kraft in the Philip Morris takeover just seven years later, but these were the first days of the big fees in the takeover business. A couple of the Marathon people were shaking their heads, and I knew what they were thinking: "How could we pay this guy all this money?" Hoopman signed the document in a very thoughtful, almost leaden way. It turned out to be a smart investment.

Pogue's sleight of hand enabled us to build the public affairs case, and that case painted Mobil in a very bad light. The strategy was to position Marathon, which happened to be a multibillion-dollar oil company, as a small, defenseless organization against Mobil, this $60 billion giant. The *Wall Street Journal* later pointed out that Mobil never based a case for its own bigness as a matter of national interest. In a nation fresh from oil shocks, it was "an argument that some legal experts term the strongest case available to the company."

We monitored the press in more than fifty cities around the world for references to the Marathon situation. We studied Marathon's whole network of outside relationships: trade connections, suppliers, even convents of nuns to which they had given money. We found countless levers to pry under the boulder of public opinion and start that opinion rolling against Mobil. In the end, if I do say so myself, the strategy worked brilliantly. Marshaling the employee and community voice of Findlay, Ohio, was the heart of our program. Here were, after all, the biggest stakeholders in the struggle.

We had to look for innovative coalitions. Ohio Senator Howard Metzenbaum had been a long-time foe of *big oil*, and Marathon was certainly *big oil*. But Mobil was *much bigger big oil*, and there were plenty of Ohio jobs riding on this roll of the dice. We called up Metzenbaum's aide and told him we were going to stage a parade rally down the main street of Findlay the next day, and wanted Senator Metzenbaum to be waving to the crowd from one of the Marathon floats. Of course, that meant a "deal." The aide wanted us to intervene on the senator's behalf and set up some contact in Washington for an Ohio industrial program. I remember the conversation distinctly: "If *you* want the senator to stand up on the back of a flat-bed truck and wave, here's what *I* want." Fortunately, putting together contacts like that is what we do. To us, it was a perfectly plausible negotiation, and we cut the deal. The next day, there was Senator Howard Metzenbaum gliding down the streets of Findlay, Ohio, shaking hands and lifting little kids onto the truck.

You could liken the parade to the victory celebration after winning a high school football championship: balloons, banners, cheering and screaming, brass bands belting out "Stars and Stripes" and "Semper Fidelis." Everywhere, there were the blank, staring eyes of video cameras. I knew that these eyes would be reporting their findings back to countless other American communities. More important, I knew that they would report the mood of Main Street back to Wall Street and, most important, Pennsylvania Avenue and Capitol Hill.

Standing next to me was Dick Cheney, Hill and Knowlton's financial maven and the man who actually coined the terms "white knight" and "poison pill." Dick pondered aloud, "I wonder what the big institutions are thinking, because they don't give a damn about hoopla." I give Dick his due, because he handled the financial dimension of the strategy masterfully, but I also knew an equally important part of this war was reaching broad public opinion, the legislators in Columbus and Washington and that wide range of noninstitutional shareholders. The plan was to make Mobil's aggression a matter of conscience, and it worked. Marathon successfully blocked Mobil's bid.

Marathon was later acquired by U.S. Steel and is now a part of USX Corporation. But, that alternative proved superior for the shareholders, the employees, and the communities affected. The Marathon takeover battle had its lessons for me:

Search for the public affairs themes in any financial crisis. They are almost always there, and they are usually powerful. Because the ownership of stock turns over so many times now, ever larger amounts of stock are in the hands of opportunistic traders. The public has more loyalty than traders and a considerable voice if it is rallied. The public expects broader accountabilities in takeovers, including to social and community interests. Also, some of those traders head up pension fund accounts and college endowments, and there are ways to bring public affairs pressure to bear on these people.

In a financial crisis, maneuver for the time necessary to forge a strong defense. The added time let us monitor information. If we hadn't monitored opinion and analyzed relationships, we could never have created as effective a plan, nor would we have adjusted it as ably as we did. Marathon had had the foresight to put together some very useful planning systems for coalitions.

Recruit old friends and use your giving record in a crisis. Marathon Oil used its corporate contributions program very skillfully in fighting and attacking Mobil. When the stock was put in play, Marathon analyzed every single corporate contribution it made for the past ten years, all the way from the Little Sisters of Charity to the Metropolitan Museum, from trade organizations to universities. From the universities, Marathon Oil brought forward professors who testified on the antitrust issue. The corporation didn't "buy" the opinions, but it found academics who held those views who were willing to speak out, because Marathon had positioned itself as an ally in the past.

Marathon activated board members and opinion leaders to argue on its behalf in both Findlay, Ohio, and the *New York Times*. Marathon also discovered which causes received contributions from its company and Mobil. It realized that it had a linkage to Mobil that could be exploited, and that's exactly what was done. Marathon "gridlocked" forces that could potentially be hostile by reminding people of Marathon's past contributions record. Had the takeover attempt happened a couple of years later, I'm sure that all this data would have been on computer, stored with this potential application in mind.

Always look for reasons why some presumed "foe" might want to be an ally in a particular case. Metzenbaum was just one case where we were able to change an adversary into an ally. We did it with labor and special-interest groups, too, in the former instance showing that their job future was safer in the hands of fellow Midwesterners than East Coast aliens.

Never ignore the power of nostalgia. There is a tremendous longing for Main Street, the marching band, and the general store. That nostalgia goes even deeper than the symbols. It supports values like craftsmanship, the workshop, local autonomy, and above all, fairness. The challenge and the opportunity are to dramatize these values in the middle of a heated contest. And that is really impossible to do unless you understand the people of a particular area, their special values and aspirations.

18

The Kansas City
Hyatt Disaster

One of the best-managed crisis situations I've ever seen was also one of the most tragic and gruesome I have ever witnessed. The two trademarks of how this crisis was handled were honesty and compassion.

On July 17, 1981, skywalks collapsed in the lobby of the Hyatt Regency Hotel across from the Crown Center in Kansas City. The walkway had been the site of a Friday tea dance in the early evening. One hundred fourteen people were killed in this accident and two hundred more were injured. Despite the awesome numbers, Hyatt managed the problem with great dignity and decency. I attribute the effectiveness with which this situation was handled to the natural instincts of the owners of the Hyatt chain, the Pritzker family, who, without injecting themselves in questions of blame, strove to communicate honestly and quickly, and to act generously at a very difficult time. It was the right way to handle a tragedy.

Once again, my wife and I had just come home from a business engagement. We'd had dinner with another couple at the Ritz Carlton in Chicago on a Friday night. We were getting ready to retire, and I picked up the ringing phone in our bedroom. On the other end was Ralph Rydholm from J. Walter Thompson, our sister ad agency. Rydholm was screaming, "Have you heard about it? Have you heard about it?

You've got to get down there! I'll get you a chartered plane."
Finally, I calmed him down and said, "Heard about what?
What's going on?" He said, "There's been a terrible disaster
at the Hyatt Hotel in Kansas City. They're our client. Would
you go down and help them right away?" I said, of course.
My next call was to let my secretary know whom I wanted to
accompany me. She rousted them up as I left for the airport.

I went out to Palwaukee, a small airport about forty
miles from the Chicago Loop, which handles commuter and
corporate jet traffic. They also had charter craft, but that
night there was only one plane left, and Ralph hadn't been
able to reserve it over the phone. We wanted it, but so did a
crew from NBC. I tipped the air service manager a hundred
bucks to take the Hill and Knowlton folks to Kansas City, and
we scurried onto the plane before the guys from the network
could make a counteroffer.

It was about three in the morning when we got to Kansas City and took a taxi to Hallmark Center. The scene had
become a cordoned-off battle zone. There was a light rainfall
as we walked up the center of the street abutting the Hyatt.
You could hear the saws cutting through the concrete and
the twisted structural steel. Despite the rain, the air was
heavy with concrete dust. I remember the eeriness of watching the wet dust splattering on our dark blue suits and a
woman colleague's London Fog raincoat. A "Twilight Zone"
unreality enshrouded everything. It must have resembled the
site of a major earthquake.

I walked over to the Westin Hotel in the same center
and called Hyatt's CEO Jay Pritzker. I woke him up; he was
trying to catch two hours of sleep in a room at the Hyatt.
Although we were both active in Chicago civic affairs, I had
never met Jay Pritzker before. He thanked us for coming and
told us to get some rest. He wanted to meet with me at 5 A.M.

Well, none of us was up for rest. We went down to look
at the site firsthand. When you see these disaster sites, you

have to steel yourself to be very objective, or else you won't be able to do your job, which is to find out the truth and present it in such a way that people can step back and look at the facts. When you see a plane crash, or a building or a bridge collapse, you quickly sense enormous physical pain. You see blood all over. You hear human cries from people who are in sustained pain. At the Hyatt, there were still victims trapped in the twisted wreckage.

With rescue experts on the scene, there is very little you can do to be physically helpful, and the worst thing you can do is to get in the way. But this inability to react physically tugs at you. Eventually, you learn to make the contribution you can make best and to stay out of the way.

The first time I saw a disaster site, it was very difficult for me. A commuter plane had crashed in Connecticut. I almost shrank from doing the job I had to do. But, I did it, albeit with great reluctance. Now, I understand when a crisis has happened, it's happened. You try to do something about it. If you can help the flow of honest and timely information, you can make a real human contribution.

Next, we went to the Hyatt Command Center and started to draw up questions we were sure the press would be asking. Extra phone lines were being installed. People were dazed. Hyatt staff members would dart out to comfort a grieving relative who'd just arrived. We wanted to start drafting plans, but we couldn't find any paper. So we wrote the questions down on McDonald's hamburger wrappers we found in a waste-paper basket.

We met with Jay and laid out our strategy in a half-hour meeting. Then we pulled together all the Hyatt people and the lawyers, and we started to get answers. Our next step was to work with the Hyatt people in conducting a series of meetings with the police, the Hallmark representatives (the greeting card company owned the center in which the hotel was located), and other groups involved. Through those meetings and our continuous monitoring of the news, locally and nationally, we developed an intelligent explanation of what had taken place—emphasizing the issues that seemed to be the foremost concerns.

The facts were that there had been a terrible disaster. We didn't know why it happened. We were working on finding that out, drawing in the best possible experts. We had great sorrow for the human loss and suffering that had occurred. We had great admiration and appreciation for the wonderful rescue workers who had come and helped. We valued the concern of the public officials and community leaders who had come to the site to make sure that everything possible was being done.

That set the tone. Everything that happened afterward was complex but straightforward. The key people at Hyatt had all been trained in crisis management. The plans were in place. The staff worked with the same kind of responsive attitude you see at Hyatt hotels under normal conditions.

As the disaster reporting unfolded over the following weeks, the structural quality of the Hyatt hotels took on topical interest for the press. Fortunately (but not unexpectedly), they were given a clean bill of health. The Hyatt hotels had long been known for their structural quality as well as their architectural innovation. Experts confirmed that the reputation was well deserved. The accident had been a bizarre and isolated construction fluke that resulted in a totally unpredictable tragedy, for which Hyatt itself had no direct responsibility.

To me, the most important impression I had amidst this grim experience was the attention that was paid to people. It made the essential difference in how people felt about the event and the company involved. The company couldn't diminish the crisis, but it did contain the aftereffects, and put the most positive possible focus on solving the problems. I think it's important to highlight those human measures:

Demonstrate compassion. Time and again, Jay Pritzker showed profound human concern. He talked constantly with the families of the dead and injured, demonstrating again and again how concerned he was. And, he genuinely was. I was so impressed by his compassion that it helped solder a human bond between the two of us that has endured since.

Bring loved ones in touch with the tragedy. The Pritzkers chartered planes to bring families of the dead and injured into Kansas City to be with loved ones, and to look at the situation. They helped overcome the space and time barriers that existed between these people and the realities they needed to face.

Use money constructively. The Pritzker family endowed a fund for the benefit of the families of people who had died in the disaster. Though many attorneys would cringe at the culpability it suggests, this was not a statement of liability. The fund went a very long way to establish the credibility of Hyatt's concern, with, incidentally, no resulting negative impact. The Pritzker family underwrote psychological help for people who were at the disaster and were so psychologically scarred that they couldn't come to grips with the situation, or their lives, afterward.

Keep reinforcing the relief efforts. The Pritzkers constantly sent letters, telegrams, and commendations to public officials and the police telling them what a great job they had done and were doing.

Managers who do the best job of managing crises are those who remember that they are first of all human beings. They feel empathy. They express compassion. They set an urgent, thoughtful standard and style that their organization is proud to emulate. And, they also find that they have the best odds of being believed and trusted. A feigned sincerity is never any substitute for simple honesty. But you should never forget that nine times out of ten, managers who are absolutely honest and straightforward in a crisis, but fail to show compassion, will not be believed.

19

Three-Mile Island: The Noncrisis

Perhaps the most celebrated *non*crisis I've ever dealt with was Three-Mile Island. I say noncrisis because outside of miscommunication nothing of material importance happened there. At least, not to the world outside the plant. While nothing of substance occurred to the public during the Three-Mile Island crisis, momentous and incredibly expensive consequences resulted from the event. First, there has been the costly cleanup of the plant itself. Second, one powerful nuclear generating unit has been shut down forever. Third, and most important, an entire industry suffered a critical setback. Not a single new nuclear plant has been opened since this event. But, the miscommunication at Three-Mile Island was the most monumental I have ever witnessed in business, and itself caused a crisis of epic proportions.

At 9:30 A.M. on Wednesday, March 28, 1979, I was in my Chicago office reviewing a client presentation. The night before, my wife and I had been out to see a newly released Jane Fonda–Jack Lemmon movie entitled *The China Syndrome*. The film's topic was a nuclear power plant disaster. I remember walking out of the theater thinking about the plot and the public relations complications that such an event would bring about. Since nuclear power utilities were among our clients, I was also considering the alarm the movie itself

165

would raise for these utilities and how they would deal with this dose of hostile opinion. As it turned out, my fantasy had a funny way of prefiguring reality. I had no idea that within hours my random thoughts would be focused on an incident of deep-reaching significance.

About five minutes into the presentation, Kate Connelly, on the Chicago staff, interrupted to ask if I had heard the news that there had been a major nuclear power plant disaster. Serious operating problems had led to a malfunction at the Three-Mile Island nuclear power plant in Middletown, Pennsylvania, not far from Harrisburg, the state capital. The extent of damage or hazard was unknown.

The first step I took was to track down Dick Hyde, our leading expert both on crisis and on the utilities industry. He also understands like no one else I know how to mount a campaign. He's like a master organist who knows just when to pull the right stops: when to invoke the media, when to "showcase" the lawyers, when to play the intelligence game. Yet, he's so low-key that he doesn't intimidate or trigger people's suspicions.

Dick understood the personal risk that might be involved at Middletown. He immediately took a train to the disaster site. When he got there, camera crews and reporters from around the world were beginning to congregate. There was great confusion and fear, including the many who doubted their own wisdom in covering this story.

At the time, we worked for Pennsylvania Electric Association. Metropolitan Edison, the utility directly involved, was a member of the Association. Metropolitan Edison called the shots on communication strategy and didn't decide to retain us until one week into the accident. By then, the communications situation was completely out of control.

There *was* a crisis at Three-Mile Island, but it was not one of nuclear safety. It was one of communication. What we know as the Three-Mile Island disaster would not have been etched into the American memory had Metropolitan Edison management given the proper level of communications direction. In the interim, local, state, and federal officials filled the knowledge void with misinformation, which in turn prompted a major-league public panic.

Metropolitan Edison's management could have moved into the breach and addressed the problem, but they didn't do it. They said that they were waiting for answers from the top managers of the parent company, General Public Utilities. Ultimately, Bill Kuhns of G.P.U. and *his* number-two man, Herman Dieckamp, had to come in and take over the job. By then it was much too late. I don't think the players in the local utility realized they could have turned it around in the first two days. The whole press communications effort was not thought through. The early press conferences had a circus atmosphere, and there was no effort made to stay in touch with the tone of press sentiment between meetings. The problem was blown way out of proportion. The hydrogen bubble—believed poised to explode—was not a real threat. No level of radioactivity exceeding permissible limits was ever discharged.

Why did the people who could have done something wait? I suspect that they thought it was smarter to wait and see if things would just go away. They didn't recognize the importance of rapidly explaining what had or had not actually happened.

Day after day, we hammered away at the people at the utility to come to a decision to do something for their community, to get clear information out. And day after day, they sat frozen. The photographs in the press were appalling. They resembled refugee lines in World War II. People were living off bottled water and canned food. There was an exodus. They packed their cars and their campers with everything they could, and jammed the highways: babies bundled in blankets, kids with scarves wrapped across their faces to limit their exposure to the "radiation," and pregnant women in sheer panic about the future they might be facing. There was a strong predisposition to ring the alarm bell.

For a decade and a half, environmentalists worldwide had made the topic of nuclear power an issue of steady controversy. The Lemmon–Fonda movie made people more receptive to reports of a nuclear power catastrophe. This situation was not unlike Orson Welles' "War of the Worlds" radio program on a Halloween night in the 1930s. The world was then just beginning to think of the possibility of space travel. H. G. Wells had written about it. Buster Crabbe's "Flash Gordon" serials were the special attraction of Saturday-afternoon matinees. The public was ready to turn fiction into reality. In Welles' case, six million heard, and over one million believed. Tens of millions were now believing the myth of Three-Mile Island.

As is the case with crises that could truly have been averted, you will always find seemingly innocent factors that helped bring the crisis into being. Look for them first in the public mood. It happened with Three-Mile Island. When there is a strong bias to believe in a disaster, a crisis can ignite with the slightest prompting.

The press had its agenda, too. When the reality of Three-Mile Island became clear, that indeed there was no threat, some of the press persisted in using it as a publicity opportunity. At one point, a reporter for one of America's most influential dailies, in a closed-door discussion with one of our people, said that he had the data that would show the problem was not serious, and that he did not intend to use it.

Government was a contributor to the problem, too. All levels of government were involved, but there was no coordinated effort. Instead of determining if evacuation was necessary, authorities publicized the different alternatives for achieving it. Doubtless, the lack of a sensibly thought-through disaster plan contributed to the mayhem. And, communications planning was totally absent. Neither Met Ed nor the

U.S. Nuclear Regulatory Commission had a workable communications disaster plan in place.

Was it fear? I'm not sure. Was it malice? I don't know. I do know that the net effect of all this disorder was to derail an industry with billions invested, and to undo its strategic plan for billions more to spend. And, it was all unnecessary.

My Jane Fonda movie experience was not the only premonition I had about Three-Mile Island. Earlier, I had gone to Middletown with Blaine Fabian, who was then manager of communications services for Met Ed. In our hardhats, we walked through the construction zone of the as-yet-unfinished cooling towers. Later, when we were back in his office, we were talking about risks facing the industry, and I said, "One day there could be a very serious issue here." Blaine leaned back in his chair smiling. He chided me not to be silly. "This is a fail-safe system," he boasted. When I asked the question, the reliability of the technology was on my mind. It was reliable. In the end, however, equal planning and thought should have been given to human communication and management judgment. The mammoth costs to the industry were every bit as high as if operational failure were the villain. Three-Mile Island remains the most powerful example of crisis communications gone awry I have ever directly experienced. What was learned from the Three-Mile Island episode? I came away with three big lessons on how to solve a problem like this one:

Tell it all and tell it fast. It's been said before, but it bears repeating. If that rule alone had been followed, there would have been no crisis.

Organize all the power centers early on. The crisis came about because there was such disarray among all the "authorities" who were dealing with the press. In a crisis, you should seek as much coordination as possible.

State your position in terms of the public interest. Almost everyone involved had a legitimate concern for the public interest, but the separate groups made their starting points defensive ones: What do we need to say to avoid being made accountable for this problem? No one saw the public interest as a point of common concern. Had they, there would have been little disagreement about either what to do or what to say.

Part V

THE POWER OF THE MEDIA

20

Hot Type and NASA Mobs

This book is about influence and power. The media, especially the big important media, cannot be influenced. Don't
try. It will backfire every time. But the media can be understood. And if you do that you can be successful as you
advance your own agenda.

While it's a delusion to think you can influence the press
in the sense of "controlling" it, you must recognize that the
press has its *own* influence. This is influence on a tremendous scale, and you gain great benefit if the influence of the
press is on your side. Successful managers can and should
project their own agenda through the press, and they must
know the rules for press contact.

I grew up with the press. Red Motley, the publisher of
Parade magazine, and columnist Drew Pearson, the precursor
of Jack Anderson, were regulars in my parents' home. My
father would come back from meetings with Scripps Howard
editors armed with piles of handouts that Jack Howard would
give his people, position papers that would argue, Should we
endorse Stevenson or Eisenhower? Was it right to invoke the
Taft–Hartley labor law injunctions? Why was Sputnik such a
serious blow to U.S. prestige?

I learned about the working world of newspaper publishing even more directly. Even though I was only ten years

old at the time, I'll never forget one particular strike threat-ened by the seven unions on the *Columbus Citizen* (which later became the *Citizen Journal*). Bargaining had gone toe-to-toe until 1:00 A.M. My dad had taken me down to the shop floor. Perhaps he wanted me to see the cunning at work in the negotiations, as he pled to keep the presses rolling. That night I learned the meaning of "being had"—but not as my dad had expected.

One of the linotype operators spotted me and punched out my name on his machine. I admired it on the setting block, and he gave the type to me with his gloved hand. I should have seen behind his too-warm smile, because of course the type was hot, and it scorched my fingers. It took all I had not to cry out, but I didn't. And I told my dad about it only years later. Today, when I hear business leaders complain that they have been "burned by the press," I laugh to myself. In my case it was literally true.

My early encounters with the press also taught me about the price tags associated with integrity. There was a depart-ment store in Columbus called Cousins and Fern. Some years ago, the owners faced a scandal when a family member committed suicide. The family begged the newspaper not to report it as such. They wanted it reported as a natural death. When the paper's editors resisted, the family threatened to pull all of the Cousins and Fern ads from the paper. They wanted the obit reporter to mask the story. The paper, how-ever, wasn't cowed, and refused. Thirty years later, the store owners have carried out their threat: Not a line of Cousins and Fern advertising appeared in the *Columbus Citizen Journal* in all the years until the store shut its doors in Columbus.

In graduate school, I did my master's thesis (in crisis communications) on NASA. I considered the Space Race the most interesting event in the world at that time, and I wanted to be right in the middle of it. I spent a lot of time in Mission Control both in Houston at the Manned Spacecraft Center, and also at what was then called Cape Kennedy. At this key moment in American history, science and government had come together. Jack Kennedy had said we were going to put a man on the moon. Space became *the* national story, and the press was there in force to cover it.

There were literally thousands of press people on the space beat. I watched them. I interviewed them. I studied them. I must have been a pest to some of them, and some were surly old hands, who didn't want to be pestered. From afar, I admired Bill Hines, then the science reporter for the *Washington Star*. Hines was a terrific writer, but he could be very abrupt with people. One day I collected my courage, and asked him, "Mr. Hines, could I have five minutes of your time? I have some questions about style I want to ask you." He snarled back that he didn't have five minutes to waste on me. Then, a few minutes later, he came back over and spent two memorable hours with me.

I was at NASA command watching the Gemini VI mission when the two astronauts were having a hard time in space. For technical reasons, the communications had suddenly blacked out, and an alarmed nation thought that the astronauts had literally been lost in space. NASA then shut down the flow of information to the press. Ben Cate from *Time* magazine stood up on a chair, took off one of his Weejun loafers, and pounded on a desk screaming that NASA was withholding information. He said that he was going to lead the reporters down the hall to break down the door of the NASA public information office. The reporters all cheered, and it felt like the French Revolution. Fortunately, NASA resumed communications; otherwise I'm certain there would have been a riot. The astronauts, I'm happy to report, were safe.

In later years, I got to see the press from all different angles: as a business and as an institution, as a crusader and as an annoyance. If the early exposure gave me one thing, it was detachment, a handy attitude for someone in my business.

175

From the very start of my career as a communicator, I've been able to look at the press with detachment and a mechanic's understanding of how it works.

The press is a major player in valuing your company. If you are a senior manager, the press also is a factor in valuing your career. The press interprets and provides the view people accept—or at least consider.

The press expects you to be out after your own interest. If you don't understand and compensate for this, the press will go to great lengths to emphasize the vested interest they will find in everything you say or do. As a result of this attitude, you may be tempted to retaliate. Don't. Crusading against the press in general or even in a particular publication is dangerous business. A hostile press can withdraw your charter to do business. The press has also become sharper and more analytical in recent years. It is dangerous for amateurs to deal with the press. Managers must understand the basics of how the press shapes power and how they should manage their business and their career with regard to the press:

Understand its three levels. The first thing you have to know about the press is that it works on three levels: publishing, editing, and reporting. Too often managers consider only the reporters.

Publications are businesses, and as such they have their own strategies. Any businessperson should begin by understanding the business objectives of the press with which he is dealing: What market are they trying to reach? How do they want to differentiate themselves from their competition? What is their business strategy for the future?

Usually, only senior executives get to know the press personally, at the publisher or business level. For senior executives, it's essential to have those kinds of ties. If you're not yet at a top level, it's still important that you read articles that give you background on the economics of the press. If you understand the economic and strategic direction of the press, you will understand editorial direction much better. The notion that business and editorial decisions in the press and media are totally separate is largely a myth.

Second, there is the editorial level, which itself really has two parts. The senior editors set direction and policy. Again, most businesspeople rarely come into contact with that level. It's more likely that managers will meet the functional editors, which may mean the business editor at their hometown paper or the editor who follows their particular specialty or industry. If you have regular dealings with the press, make a point of knowing who the editors are as well as the reporters, particularly if there are different reporters following your company, depending on the day's assignments. The editor can also be your point of appeal if a particular reporter persistently reports on you unfairly. If an unknown person calls contending to be a reporter for a particular publication, the editor is the person you contact to verify that the reporter is legit.

Learn the economics of the press. Television, changing media habits, clutter, and a host of other developments are rewriting the economics of publishing the news. Newspaper circulation has remained essentially flat since the beginning of the 1970s.

Forbes reports that newspapers are diversifying into data bases and other media businesses. For the first time in decades, magazines may be relying more on circulation than on advertising as their principal source of revenue. But the press is not a pauper yet. The revenues of the *Washington Post* exceed the combined gross national product of Nicaragua and El Salvador!

Study how the press shapes its opinions. The classic editorial writer's strategy parallels that of a marketer trying to attack the leading firm in his industry. Both will look for one or more weaknesses in the leader's purported strengths. Successful editorialists never attack a total position. They almost always attack one small element, often a parenthetical phrase in a seemingly unimportant speech or press release. Andy Chancellor, a retired writer on the Hill and Knowlton staff, wrote hundreds of editorial and op-ed pieces springing off just this maneuver.

When a company is the target of an opinion piece, I usually recommend counting to ten and then forgetting about it. Hours are spent on letters to the editor or on analyzing what went wrong, but the future is what counts. People are obsessed with the past. They want to get revenge. Maybe it's a way to work out frustration. But, I've seen an awful lot of pencils broken. And in almost every instance, all you get for your efforts are bad feelings from the media. It's always best to avoid spear-throwing contests with journalists.

Still, managers need to understand how journalists develop their own opinions, how they project them, and how their approach is changing. Don't go to the editorial pages of business publications to learn how the press looks at business. After all, the editorial position of all major business publications is automatically pro-business. To learn the important changes in the way editorials are written today, I suggest looking at the general press.

John Seigenthaler is editorial page editor for *USA Today* and has a good sense for how the press has to package opinion differently today than a decade or two ago. He points out five ways in which press editorialists must approach their task differently in the 1990s. I think that the same principles and concerns hold for anyone trying to persuade through the written word, including companies and individual managers.

Respect the reader's time shortage. John Seigenthaler believes that "The key problem confronting readers is the absence of time to absorb a viewpoint." Through a host of sources, they've already gotten the news, albeit in chunks. They want someone to tie the basics together efficiently, and give them a sensible outlook on the problem.

Shape "softer," more subtle attacks. Readers are "no longer convinced by hammer-head polemics," says Seigenthaler. They are weary of and immune to an emotionally charged style on most issues. That's how editorialists in papers are doing it. That's how managers should do it, too, when they write opinion pieces for their company publications.

Expect more "crusading journalism" from television. "Editorialists today are less given to crusading," Seigenthaler observes. "They are more comfortable with presenting balanced argumentation." The trend is toward laying out the essential evidence, with the understanding that readers are more comfortable today drawing their own conclusions. Much of the crusading on personal causes is shifting to TV, because TV is so much more graphic. You see it on such shows as "Inside Edition" or "A Current Affair." Whereas the national publications, magazines, and papers have backed off from crusades, many local papers are still involved. Author John Taylor has called the print version of this kind of journalism "cheesecake and mayhem." The stories covered on the derivative TV shows—the towns victimized by cults or bullies, the village crusading against a developer, or the business exposed for its exploitation—are often stories unearthed by local newspapers. On the big issues, though, television sets the general press agenda much as the trade press sets the agenda for the general business press.

Use print to verify and explain. In political campaigns, Seigenthaler sees other evidence of television's increasing importance. "The action is being shared today between the print and the electronic journalists," he believes. In my opinion, it's going to television. In 1988, the newspapers essentially covered the fairness and effectiveness of the television campaign. That means to me that managers better look at their print communication in a new light. Its ongoing value may be to explain or verify the messages and symbols management creates in person or by video. When it comes to forming and influencing opinions, print is now secondary communication.

Anticipate the hostile attitudes toward business held by much of the press. Editorial writers still have a problem with business, but industry leaders often do themselves a disservice by the way they present their case. Businesspeople need a more informed and intelligent attitude toward the press. John Seigenthaler sees it this way: "The businesspeople who are most successful with the press are the ones who find out how it works, really works. The bad ones don't really want to know. They may hire good communications counsel and then neglect to use it. They still believe you can 'fix' the press. They are the kind who lecture reporters at press conferences. Their attitude vacillates between hostility and naivete."

———

There are some special points to consider when dealing with the roughly 2,800 trade publications and business papers in the United States. Each week some die; every day it seems a new one is born. Many have negligible influence. They are contrived by opportunistic publishers simply as advertising vehicles. But, the important trade publications have quite a different role. They are often the recognized statistical sources of their industries. They provide annual rankings of business volume, profitability, and other measures of scope and effectiveness. In my profession, Jack O'Dwyer's newsletter on public relations certainly occupies that role.

If you want to see how powerful the trade press can be, take a look at the construction industry. In that industry, which is the largest in the United States, there are few authorities more respected than Art Fox, the recently retired head of construction's leading trade publication, *Engineering News-Record*. Any manager in business will want to know and understand the Art Foxes of the world and how their publications work.

Sound ties with the trade press are the heart of any healthy relationship with the press. All of the mainstream, national publications in this country do a lot of primary research, but they also rely heavily on trade publications and local papers to help them identify up-and-coming stories. Since only 36 percent of top executives depend on their own local paper for their business news, managers often reject local coverage as unimportant to their own future or the future of their firms. That's a grave mistake. Attitudes are even worse toward trade journals, which seem so familiar and mundane to managers. That attitude is both shortsighted and costly.

Respect the indispensability of the trade press. Art Fox believes that the best trade journals are essential, which means that "If any of the biggest mass circulation business magazines disappeared tomorrow, its share would be gobbled up by the others that remained, and by the *Wall Street Journal*. If one of those disappeared, no one would remember after a month or two. If *Engineering News-Record* or *Aviation Week* disappeared, another publication just like it would emerge overnight.

"The specialized trade press has a certain unique indispensability to it. We may provide information that is closer to the executive's bottom-line threats and opportunities than our general press counterparts do. We also work harder to get that information than many might think. When the Pentagon unveiled the new B-2 Stealth bomber, there were rigid restrictions on how close photographers could get to the plane. *Aviation Week* hired an airplane to shoot aerial photographs. These were the only top-down profiles of the plane anyone had gotten. No one in the general press felt the need to try that hard."

If you want to know an industry's agenda, look for it in its leading trade publication. The trade press takes on the silhouette of what is important to any particular industry. The general press must constantly educate the casual reader on the meanings of terminology and concepts. The trades needn't do so. Fox explains, "One of the great advantages of trade publications is their efficiency. They don't strive to be jargon-ridden, but neither do they have to clarify every concept. That means they can deliver an excellent information return for the time that is invested in reading them."

Understand how the trades interpret breaking news for the public. The trades also play a more important role today in helping to explain aspects of breaking news to their industry and to the general media. When the Mexico City and Armenian earthquakes occurred, *Engineering News-Record* dispatched correspondents and talked to visiting experts, as it would for any event of this sort. Fox says that trades have an important role in assisting the general media. "Networks and newspapers are in touch with us," he says, "to get a better understanding of the technical problems in such disasters. During Vietnam, there was a great deal of new construction—roadways and air strips—and a large contingent of civilian engineers and technicians directing it. As a result, we became war correspondents. When our industry intersects with general news, we often become the Rosetta stone to explain what is happening."

The trade press also has growing direct authority with a broader public. At the very least, its influence is felt with opinion leaders. When the *New England Journal of Medicine* or *Lancet* publishes a controversial new finding, you can bet it's headline news on the networks in hours. It's reported because the media have learned that trade journal stories are important in influencing opinion. In 1988, a purported account of euthanasia in the *Journal of the American Medical Association* ignited a national debate that raged for days. An anonymous doctor had confessed to inducing the death of a terminally ill young cancer victim. Because it appeared in *JAMA*, it had an authority beyond dispute and actually set the national agenda for a debate on mercy killing.

The distance between the specialized and trade publications and the general public is constantly diminishing. That's due in part to more and more people becoming specialists in the general work force; they understand the need for specialized input.

Use the trade press's natural friendly feelings to your advantage. It's easier to maintain a friendly relationship with the trade press than the general press. After all, the trade press relies on its company relationships for all-important access to information. Almost any firm should be able to maintain a positive relationship with the leading trade publications in their industry. It's just not that hard, and it can be very useful. Any failure to do so is usually a clear signal of a badly bungled press relations program. Many of the things I have said above also hold true for the local press. Both are important in their own right and are certainly power channels to the mainstream, national business press.

21

How to Look at Reporters ... and Get Them to Run Your Story

A couple of years back, Campbell Soup learned on a Wednesday that there would probably be a hostile story about them in the *Wall Street Journal*. They thought that they would try to angle for an article in *Business Week* to get out the Campbell side of the story. So the company pushed ahead toward that goal and spent a load of man-hours. Unbeknownst to Campbell, they had a big problem: *Business Week* "closes its book" at noon on Thursday. Campbell could have opened every file in the company and it would have never made it into the publication. Our telling them the simple deadline fact turned off the spigot on the waste.

David Gergen is now editor-at-large for *U.S. News and World Report*. Hedrick Smith relates that Gergen says of his approach as a speech writer in the White House, "Before any public event was put on [Nixon's] schedule, you had to know what the headline out of that event was going to be, what the picture was going to be, and what the lead paragraph would be." Any manager who conducts press relations with that kind of discipline is likely to win more often than not.

According to Carol Loomis, who sits on *Fortune*'s editorial board, "Saying no to the press is not the ultimate sin. Failing to return phone calls within a reasonable time *is*. Failing to return phone calls is a form of arguing. I would be very mindful of an old rule which says: Never argue with a man who buys ink by the barrel."

Obviously, you should pay attention to deadlines, headlines, and telephone lines! But never neglect the human element. Reporters are the press contact point most managers get to know. Here are some guidelines to maximize your effectiveness with reporters:

Don't try to con a reporter or a publication. Managers and companies can manipulate the press, but you have to be very good to do it, and you can't do it for very long. Don't pretend to know things you don't. Don't speculate without the proper background. Don't try to manipulate the press. The foundation of your influence with the press is credibility.

When you agree to an interview, check out the reporter. Believe me, that reporter will check you and your company out as thoroughly as he possibly can. Most reporters for major business publications are reputable. However, some are not. Use your communications department to help you decide which is which. If you have a data base, retrieve articles the reporter has written. Does he or the publication have an "agenda" on your company or your industry? Ask someone on your communications staff to call up other companies about which the reporter or publication has written. Do they feel they were treated fairly? Were off-the-record and not-for-attribution conditions upheld?

Watch out for reporters who suddenly shift publications. Why did they make the move? You'll want to know if a reporter has the reputation of being turbulent or erratic. A story in a major publication can have as much impact on you as the departure of a key executive. A story can disrupt your stock price or your company morale or your acquisition plans.

There are even directories that can help you check out reporters. Jude Wanniski publishes an annual *Media Guide* in which he indexes 2,000 reporters nationwide. Dean Rotbart of TJFR (*The Journalist and Financial Reporting*) offers a *Business News Atlas* which provides organization charts of leading business newsrooms. With the globalization of business, I expect someone will soon publish an international directory of reporters. But, if you are making serious preparation for an interview, you must go further than checking background and credentials. Read the articles and look at the words a reporter uses to describe certain issues.

Think about why he uses those words: Do they reflect a certain bias? Is there a technical aspect of your industry that the reporter doesn't understand that you could clarify for him? What provokes warmth and admiration in the reporter's stories? What does he seem to like, and how can you trigger those reactions?

Research the background and motives of reporters doing a story as carefully as you would those of a management candidate you are about to hire. Some reporters can do a remarkable job of cloaking their motives, even from their editors. An intriguing case in point is that of A. Kent MacDougall, a business reporter who worked for the *Wall Street Journal* and the *Los Angeles Times* for about twenty years. In 1989, MacDougall announced that he was a socialist and that he occasionally used his assignments to publicize his radical views. Careful reading of MacDougall's pieces would have exposed his bias. But less pronounced viewpoints, which can still shade a story, may go completely unnoticed unless you read the articles and do the research. To understate it, not many business reporters in the United States are socialists, but there are many other idiosyncrasies that can influence a story. If you know these up front, there are things you can do to tailor your message and your presentation.

Help the reporter to understand your business or industry. Reporters are journalists, not operating executives. Taking time to give them some background can make their work a lot easier. Kraft has done a terrific job of educating reporters who follow the food industry. Sometimes just twenty minutes spent by a top-ranking person to explain a difficult concept can create a lifelong positive relationship.

Be available to reporters when they are doing stories that aren't about your company. Look at your dealings with the press as relationships. You need to establish credibility with reporters and publications over time. They may want to talk about a very routine press release, not a breakthrough announcement of a new product, but it may tie into some other story they are working on. Make a point of being available for the commonplace. If reporters call looking for insight or reactions when a major news event breaks, or they are doing an industry roundup, cooperate. If you are dealing with a reputable reporter—and the vast majority are reputable—you can always do so off the record.

Always treat a reporter with the respect you would accord any human being . . . who is also a potential adversary. Be friendly and upbeat with the reporter, never arrogant or overbearing. *Never* be rude, because that rudeness will often be directly transmitted to the viewing or reading audience. But, also never forget that it's the reporter's job to discover interesting, unique, and controversial information. Never let the reporter's appetite for the interesting get in the way of your goal.

Companies can have much more power in steering the press than they realize. You can't "fix" the press, but you can leverage your position. Often, a simple change in contact style and knowledge of a few basic facts will improve press relations substantially.

When you want to sell a story to the press, draw the picture in the first sentence. Reporters are always receptive to good story angles, but they get a huge volume of suggestions. If you can get right to the point, you help them and you help yourself. (The same is true when you are telling your story to a print or an electronic journalist. The time frame, especially for broadcast reporting, is so compressed that you must get your message out in the first words you speak.)

Line up sources to support your reputation or your story. Reporters regularly consult and cite authoritative sources in their articles. These authorities bolster credibility. It's possible to identify who many of these people are, and sometimes to "position" them so that the press will be likely to contact them. They include analysts, industry consultants, researchers, trade journalists, and other executives in your industry. One of the best reasons for not bad-mouthing your competition to the press is that if you do, your competitors will wait anxiously for the day they can return the favor. It's easy to build bridges to all these other authorities, except perhaps competing executives.

You may be able to wire a reporter on a publication into some of the voices useful to bolstering your own position. A casual mention in a phone call or interview is how you do it. "I had a really tough time persuading Jack Nimrod, the analyst, at Melbourne & Sweet that we were on the right strategic course, but now he says that he really buys what we're doing." Or, "Margaret Thomas was one of our best marketing executives, and we were very sorry to lose her to a competitor. When I spoke with her last month, she said our firm was the best possible training ground she could have had for being president of her new company." The odds are the reporter will try to reach those people.

Design the story you want written. Companies will go through endless drafts of press releases about such important issues as reorganizations or new strategies. Few have the discipline to "write" the story you want written. Have someone on your staff with solid journalistic experience and a good dose of realism do that job. Actually draft a story as you would want it to appear. That experienced professional will also keep you honest. He'll know those dodges that no credible journalist will ever accept as an explanation or interpretation. Write the releases, plan the interviews, and design the anticipated questions-and-answers backgrounder so as to "produce" the story you hope will be written. You will be surprised at how much this discipline will improve your aim.

Choose the negatives that will be written about you. Many managers remain naive perfectionists. They believe that they can actually have a major story written about them or their company without negatives or at least without questions being raised. One of the first principles of journalism is balance. No matter how perfect any company may look, a journalist will automatically dig for the questionable and sobering angles on the story. He is obliged to find some meaningful flaws. When most companies prepare for a story, they spend all their time trying to package what they hope to hype. They think about the negatives as things to hide. Instead, they should think about what negatives they want to let emerge and how they will explain them, so they have credibility. If a company steadfastly conceals its faults, you can be sure that a reporter will run to outside sources to have faults produced. Would you rather be in charge of deciding what your faults are, or be victimized by someone else's phantoms or exaggerations?

Stay out of the spotlight. That may sound like curious advice from a communications counselor, but I earnestly recommend avoiding feature stories about you or your company. If you actively pursue a major story on your company, you could be asking for serious trouble. I can count on one hand the number of times I believe seeking out feature publicity worked for the benefit of the firm doing it. The usual effect is a big question mark about the rightness of the company's decisions and direction.

If you're the target of a major story, expect the press to go everywhere. We just represented a client about whom the *Wall Street Journal* talked to better than 400 people in the process of developing a story. The reporters talked to family members, teachers of the CEO's kids, analysts, other press people, local reporters, former employees, even groups the company supported with donations. There is a huge reservoir of sources beyond your company. Expect it will be tapped, and do what you can to align probable sources to your agenda.

Never forget that good news begets bad news. Campbell Soup affords a great case in point. In December 1984, there was a glowing article about Campbell's in *Business Week*. It talked about Campbell's highly innovative market niche strategy, how they were pursuing the Hispanic market, young actives, and a host of other well-defined niches. I have no idea if it was sought-after publicity or not. The point is it was big marketing news.

January 1987 rolled around and the Campbell Soup Kids, dressed up like yuppie executives, were on the cover of *Business Week* as symbols of "marketing's new look." Then, in the next month, *USA Today* ran a cover story with praise ringing from the rafters. What happened? A lot of people were waiting to write the antistory, and it happened. In July 1988, the *Wall Street Journal* devoted a lengthy section of its "Who's News" column to "Campbell ... struggling to pull itself out of the soup," under the header that the firm "is quietly seeking [an] outsider to succeed" the CEO. A month and a half later, *Forbes* did a feature with the title (based on a quote from the CEO) "We're not running the company for the stock price." Over the title was the header "Campbell Soup Co. still makes the vegetable and tomato soups much as it did seventy years ago. That's one of its problems." In September 1989, *Business Week* itself came full circle on Campbell with an article titled "M'm! M'm! Bad! Trouble at Campbell Soup." Campbell is still a very well-respected firm, and is well on its way back. Today, they are pursuing a much more deliberate policy with the press. They may not have gone out of their way to get any of the earlier publicity, but their experience shows the peril of high visibility in the press. Very few firms can count on an ever-rising stream of earnings or product successes.

If you garner highly visible praise, you're likely to provoke highly visible raspberries once you slip. Who will ever forget the *Business Week* cover story follow-up on the forty-three firms celebrated in *In Search of Excellence? Business Week* found fourteen of them suffering from a loss of "luster" just two years later. Nobody likes a hero.

Develop a constant, positive, and low-key press presence.
"My competition is always in the press, but we're never there."
That is a complaint I often hear. Invariably, that happens
because the competition makes itself available. The competition has figured out the four or five columns and regular
features where its company or industry will be commented
on: the tax column or the "Labor Letter" in the *Wall Street
Journal*; the technology page in the *New York Times*; or the
media page in the *Los Angeles Times*. Smart companies go to
the editors and reporters of those columns and say, "Look, I
know you're not going to write about my company every day.
I don't want you to. But, you are going to write about the
industry, and I'm available to give you background information, quotes, industry figures, and trend data." Identify the
big columns that impact your business. Monitor them for a
couple of months. Take a yellow highlighter and identify the
companies mentioned. I guarantee you those are the sources
inside the industry upon whom the publications and reporters rely.

Slip under the microscope once a year. If your company
hungers to be above the fold on the front page of the Sunday
New York Times "Business Section," then you should know
you're living dangerously. Of course, it doesn't hurt to be
cited in roundup stories of the "best managed" or "most
successful" companies, provided you don't use this to fuel
more big-piece coverage. Smaller companies, which have a
greater motivation to be recognized, especially by Wall Street,
may have slightly more justification to go after publicity. But
they should do it very carefully.

Every major business publication keeps a list. If you're a
Fortune 500 company, you will generally be a topic for each
of them once a year. Your objective should be to let the
episode pass as painlessly as possible. Let some innocuously
newsworthy event be the peg of the story, a new product or a

new market you're entering. You want the coverage on your terms, not the publication's terms. You have to know the thirty-eight different ways that will get you into *Business Week.* You must then choose the least onerous way. You had also better realize that you're probably going to take a pasting from one of the three or four top publications, *especially* if everyone else loves you. Again, you want even a hatchet job to be as much on your terms as possible. Be big enough to understand that someone will try to take the knife to you. Remember, a negative angle on even the best-run business sells papers and magazines.

Don't assume the reporter will write a story. Not every story that gets researched gets written. Reporters react to plausible tips, but they are also smart enough to challenge tips and leads. Perhaps the source is a disgruntled former employee. Maybe, it's a supplier who's nursing a grudge. It could be that a mischievous competitor or a plotting congressional staff member is trying to set you up.

In almost all cases, you will have the opportunity to persuade a reporter that a story doesn't exist. To do this, you can use various tactics. If you aren't quite ready to reveal a major breakthrough, consider rewarding the reporter for his skill in spotting a story that might be there. Tell him that if he holds the story, the particulars of which you can't confirm right now, you will give him "exclusive access" to details and background. This delaying tactic may work for weeks, but not for months. If several other reporters fall on the same scent quickly, the gambit won't work, and with some reporters, that kind of deal making won't work at all.

If there really is no story, just speculation or innuendo, you can often shut it down by being open and discussing the facts. Reporters, especially those for reputable business publications, don't want to embarrass themselves by writing fiction.

Finally, there might indeed be a story, but one that includes a host of explanations and mitigating factors. Nothing discourages a journalist more than rampant confusion that he can't explain to his readers. You must draw a fine but important distinction. If the confusion and the several plausible interpretations are real, then by all means go ahead. However, if you just conjure up a smoke screen to keep the reporter at bay, that act may cause him to sharpen his knives with a vengeance when he discovers what you have done.

Never string out a big, bad story in the hopes it will go away. Watergate is the best example of this rule. If Nixon had come out in the first few days and said, "Look, this is a third-rate burglary. Here are the guys responsible. They're fired. This was an outrageous act, and I disavow it," the whole Watergate thing wouldn't have happened. By permitting the press to drag out the ordeal, it became a huge negative story.

Plan press strategy early. In any controversial arena, make press positioning an early consideration or you may do it wrong. Think about it in the first planning stages, while you still have the opportunity to influence opinion. This is true if you're on the offense or stuck in a defensive position. Saying to yourself that you'll dodge the press and deal with them only if the pressure is turned up is not a strategy. Many do this and get burned later. It's a hope and a song, and it can get you into a heap of trouble.

Be very wary of switching press tactics in midstream. For example, a manager decides to stay out of the press on an issue. The press picks up the story and it gets plenty of play. Still, the manager won't comment. The heat turns up. There's more negative publicity and management panics. The spin doctors tell management to dive in and bust the negative momentum of the press. The company leaders reverse course and consent to an interview. They think that they have smothered the blaze at the eleventh hour. But, in most cases, they have just added their endorsement to what is bound to be a negative story.

This is exactly what happened to RJR Nabisco chief F. Ross Johnson in the competitive scramble to acquire RJR Nabisco. Johnson, who was CEO of the company, was also one of the competitors seeking to buy the business in a leveraged buyout. Fearing that the press was about to turn on him, Johnson learned that *Time* was going to do a major piece, so he made an eleventh-hour agreement with *Time* to participate in an interview. The week following the interview, Johnson's picture appeared on *Time*'s cover alongside the title "A Game of Greed: This man could pocket $100 million from the largest corporate takeover in history. Has the buyout craze gone too far?"

The interview tarnished Johnson through his own quoted comments. He showed only a casual interest in the future welfare of employees affected by a takeover. The remarks added credibility to *Time*'s position, as did the photo of Johnson's smiling face. Many PR professionals believe that the *Time* story was the single decisive error that lost Johnson a $17 billion deal. I think the *Time* piece was instrumental, but what it really did was cap off all the uncertainty and negativism that preceded it, especially an article in the *New York Times*. Ross Johnson later commented in *Fortune* that the *Times* article turned the tide in favor of Kohlberg Kravis Roberts, Johnson's chief opponent in bidding for RJR. It created the villain that *Time* later magnified. Johnson himself later wrote in *Fortune*, "[The *Times* piece's appearance was] when they won the public relations war . . . it took all the attention off the greed on Wall Street and put it on me." Many factors caused Johnson's trouble, but none was as damaging as the decision to alter press strategy.

Don't plead for more sympathy than you deserve. When Texas Air faced a critical strike at its Eastern Airlines subsidiary, Texas Air CEO Frank Lorenzo stood in front of the television cameras and said how deeply the difficulty at Eastern Airlines affected him and his family. Of course the unions came back and said, "How about us and our families? We're not making Lorenzo's salary." In contrast, look how good Peter Ueberroth made himself look by drawing unions into a partnership in his attempted buyout. Time and again, Ueberroth demonstrates a remarkable skill in building consensus: in baseball, in the war on drugs, with the Olympics, and in just about everything else. You could never imagine Ueberroth feeling sorry for himself.

Take the high road and travel in the best company. When the Mike Milken scandal erupted at Drexel Burnham, look at how Drexel's CEO, Fred Joseph, saved himself. He prepared the way first by bringing in as a consultant former White House Chief of Staff Howard Baker. No one in Washington is cleaner than Howard Baker. Then Joseph recruited former SEC commissioner John Shad as Drexel's new chairman. This was shortly after Shad had pledged his $20 million for the new Harvard ethics program. Fred Joseph is still in position because he kept going in front of the press, and he kept spotlighting these appointments as decisive actions. He didn't necessarily defend Drexel, but he always took the high road. He separated himself from Milken very carefully.

Showcase support carefully with the press. When House Speaker Jim Wright was charged with wrongdoing by twelve of his House colleagues, his decision to attend a caucus with sixty-nine Democrats, before he went to the full House, was a big mistake. I can still remember him standing with his band of Democrats in front of the video cameras. He not only punctured his defense with sixty-nine potential leaks but he also made his integrity a partisan issue. The ethics committee that charged him was squarely bipartisan, but he delivered purely partisan support. In relatively short order, Wright was out of a job.

22

Rumors and Leaks, Releases and Pix

Big Brother isn't watching us yet, but managers must realize that their behavior is being constantly observed and analyzed by countless individuals inside and outside their organizations. When you're on the job, you're on camera. During his administration, President Reagan taped a weekly radio message to the public. In a now-famous moment in August 1984, he made an offhand comment as he was warming up for this talk. Not realizing the mike was on, he joked that he "just signed legislation that will outlaw Russia forever." President Reagan then said: "The bombing begins in five minutes." It didn't go out over the air, but it was overheard by technicians at stations nationwide. The press had a field day. It became a point of embarrassment in the 1984 presidential campaign. Had Reagan not had such enormous popularity, it could have cost him the election.

Reagan was not alone. The microscope or the lens is constantly trained on the president of the United States. After an operation, Lyndon Johnson pulled out his shirt to unveil a scar on his stomach. The photo made the front page of newspapers across the country. Once again, Johnson came across as a small-town Texas rube.

Both of these incidents were unnecessary lapses. The eye and ear of the media are relentlessly recording what managers say and do, probing for evidence to support one viewpoint or another, and almost always trying to prove something to the manager's detriment.

Any company that gives conflicting information or does not seem to be in control of sensitive data weakens its position. At the same time, unofficial information often has considerable power. Managers have to learn how these data flow. Outside of judicious use of "off-the-record" comments with the press, managers with long-term smarts will stay away from all other subterfuge, *especially* rumors and leaking.

Use "off the record" carefully and define exactly what you mean. Today, so much is done "off the record" or "on background" by reporters gathering information. This method can give some people a dangerous weapon: They can't pass up the chance to be critical, but they don't want to be accountable for it. Only one manager has to jump ship to a competitor and disclose that his former employer was behind all those mean-spirited quotes, and the jig is up. You become the industry cheap-shooter and earn a ton of bad will.

Going off the record to criticize direction within your own company is risky business and I would never recommend it. Nor would I recommend going off the record to do something illegal or in violation of company policy, such as forecasting earnings or disclosing material information like a contemplated major divestiture or change of strategic direction.

Going off the record is ticklish for other reasons, not the least being that the definition of "off the record" is very ambiguous. For most it means being able to give a quote to a reporter that the reporter can use but not attribute to you personally. "Not for attribution" is a synonym for going off the record. Be sure that you define with the reporter how closely an "off-the-record" or "not-for-attribution" quote is to be identified. I have known more than one executive who shot himself in the foot by giving a reporter an "off-the-record" quote. The quote ends up attributed to a "member of senior management" with the trail leading back to the manager in question. Set up clearly how the reporter is going to attribute the statements: Will you be "an unidentified source close to the company" or "a source within the company" or have some other description?

Another stipulation in a phone call or interview with a reporter is "for background only," which generally means that you are giving the reporter background information or a perspective on the company or the industry. No quotes—attributed or unattributed—are to come from that discussion.

There's one dependable rule: You should always assume that any information you give a reporter may end up published at some time. Just be sure that you clearly state what the conditions are and what they mean. Define your terms with the reporter before leaving the official record and when you return to it so you aren't surprised later.

Quash rumors coolly and then track down the source. Rumors can be a problem inside the company as well as with the press. They are a favored, underhanded weapon used to dissipate the influence of an executive. Shrewd executives, when confronted with destructive rumors about them or their business, maintain an unflappable exterior—and methodically try to track down the source of the rumors and the motive behind them.

Expect leaks to be a constant aggravation in management life. Leaks to the press of rumors within your company are the most pesky to handle. Reporters sit at their desks every day and get unsigned letters, anonymous telephone calls, and other tips that pour over the transom. Most are the work of "spoilers" who want to put your company in play or cast you or your company in a bad light. You have to realize that this is happening. Solidly built, long-term relationships with the media are your only protection against the kind of damage rumors can do.

Most "reputable" publications won't print a story unless they have it from two sources (albeit "unidentified"). But rumormongers are on to that. Two employees on the loading dock can conspire together, make separate phone calls, and bingo, suddenly your company is in play, and to prove it there's a story in the paper that Carl Icahn is chasing it.

Have a clear policy on press communications. Many companies restrict their employees' access to the press on company business. A typical disclosure policy would be, "Press inquiries are to be directed without comment to the corporate communications department. The company views information on any aspect of its business to be proprietary and not to be disclosed, except as permitted by and under the direction of the corporate communications department." I know of no company that ever got in trouble because of such a stance and I know of many who have gotten in trouble because they lacked a clear statement.

Look for the leaker's footprints. After you tell your people not to talk with the press, be realistic enough to know that some of them will. If you have a serious, straightforward policy on press relations, you won't eliminate leaks, but you should be able to contain them.

Assess the pros and cons of a leak on your agenda. Every potential story has to be evaluated this way: If it's leaked, how will it damage you? If three people know a story, assume a leak will probably occur. Ask the question, Will a leak help me? If the answer is yes, let it leak. Will it hurt me? Then get your story out as fast as possible to regain control of your agenda.

Don't treat the press release as a "corporate fig leaf." That's a term I recently heard a reporter use, and it says a lot. The purpose of a press release is *not* to cover up something unmentionable. Anything so carefully worded is guaranteed not to be believed. The press rarely uses press releases to write their stories. The amount of time that managers, lawyers, and staff spend poring over press releases to "get it right" is really wasted.

Real stories are based on real interviews with managers, and the quotes, examples, and color that the managers and authorities provide. An article is driven by the special angle the reporter can detect and create. The manager must also understand that the reporter will go to the competition and the company's enemies, analysts, industry watchers, third-party experts, and academics. If the manager is doing his job properly, he or his communications experts have lined up these sources to get as much support as they can.

Always seek a second and third opinion. You have to be careful with a press release. A bad one can blow up in your face. You should be careful to get the information right, to avoid mistakes, which is quite different from thinking you can manipulate the world through the release. Don't just rely on your own judgment. Have two, and preferably three, trusted advisors read any document before it's released. (At least one of those people should be a communications pro.)

While you should be cautious with releases, you can also be too cautious. It's a bad practice to issue a release that sounds "legalistic." A company that speaks with the voice of a lawyer has already put itself on trial. Probably nothing earns the instant contempt and suspicion of journalists more than carefully hedged comments drafted by an attorney. They are as obvious to a journalist as the difference between an actor and a nonactor on television. Lawyers have legitimate input to any major company statement, but managers have to weigh its relative value. Is the point of making the statement to have it announced or to have it believed?

———

Many managers think interviews and photos are spontaneous events, but they are only if you let them be. If you want to control how you are treated, there is no substitute for thoughtful planning.

Prepare. You have to assume that a reporter wants to create a fair story. I think that in business publications the days of slanted journalism, of "Let's go out and get these guys," are over. But that doesn't mean you'll be treated fairly if you don't do your homework.

In advance of a major interview, most senior executives are now smart enough to insist on staff preparation, which includes background on the story and anticipated questions and answers. As I've said, you should ask for background on the reporter, the publication, and its relationship to the company.

After you've done the research, your homework still isn't done: Brainstorm with your staff or your communications advisors. Talk through the objectives of the publication, consider the negatives they may want to bring up, and try to understand your company in the context of your industry and competition, which is exactly how the publication will look at you. Then, plan your own messages.

Role-play the interview. Always role-play questions and answers before a press interview with another manager, preferably one with a communications background. When you role-play, consider the toughest, nastiest, dirtiest questions you can. Doing so will make those questions less intimidating and strengthen your answers.

If you don't prepare this material exhaustively and absorb it, you are leaving yourself open to a series of questions that will be largely negative and perhaps openly critical. This obviously requires time, but it's not wasted time. I've gone through this exercise with a good number of Fortune 500 CEOs. When managers master these messages for the press, they also have them down cold for internal audiences.

Be credible. It's said often enough, but what does it mean? Basically, it means, can what you say be believed? One of the experts on communications in environmental crises, such as toxic waste spills, observes, "Reporters [in a crisis] cover viewpoints, not 'truths.' "

Truth is a very subjective matter. Competence is less subjective. Do you have enough knowledge about a subject to have an intelligent viewpoint? Otherwise, why should you be talking and why should others listen to you? Credibility means not bluffing. It means not pretending to be an expert when you are not. Every influential manager I have ever encountered knows the limits of his credibility.

If you can't talk about something, just say so. Be direct, but not hostile. "We don't talk about rumors of acquisitions," "I'm sorry, we have a firm policy not to discuss earnings," or "For reasons I can't get into here, I just can't talk about that right now."

Take the edge off "no comment." There are many legitimate times for a company to say "no comment" to the press. There are also ways to take the edge off the "no comment" statement, which sounds more like a door slam than an answer. My favorite is, "We won't have any comment until we get more details, and have had a chance to study them."

Conduct the interview alertly. Managers are spotty in the way they handle interviews. For one thing, they lose sight of the interpersonal dynamics at play. Reporters know the same trick that psychologists and recruiters who assess executives have long grasped. They all know that interviews are pressure situations. The most telling insights into the people being interviewed come when the subject is off-guard.

Dismiss the outrageous. If the reporter asks a question that is totally out-of-line or absurd, control your anger. You might get a left-field question or comment like, "Your colleagues say that your strongest motivation is your deep-seated personal hatred for your chief competitor's chairman," "Your wife consults a fortune-teller, doesn't she?" or "Why do you get such a great personal pleasure out of demeaning your predecessor?" Dismiss the seriousness of such remarks. Use rejoinders like, "You can't be serious," and "I won't even dignify that question with an answer. Now, let's get back on course."

Decide in advance if you will let the reporter tape you. There are many different viewpoints on the use of tape recorders. Some reporters don't use them because they can be a crutch. They contend their minds wander in the interview, trusting they "can go back and find out everything later." Recordings are usually not harmful if you are an executive who reins in his emotions and isn't prone to outbursts. If it's a major piece, if the company is in a sensitive situation, or if the reporter is reputed to be a "cad," it's smart policy to simultaneously record the conversation for your own records. Some managers feel badly inhibited by a tape recorder. That's a factor to consider, too. When you are talking for background or off the record, make sure the reporter's machine is turned off.

Think "visually" about the press. The visual dimension of the press can be both hazard and opportunity. Because of the way television has changed how we look at the printed page, more than ever before, the press wants graphic excitement. You have to understand the press needs to enliven their pages with more than just gray type.

When a manager or a company worked with the press in the past, words and ideas were the first-place considerations. Today, equal attention should be paid to the pictures and images. What kind of specially made-up graphs and charts could you give the press? What really unique photographs or photo opportunities can you offer? What other kinds of visuals—graphs, bar charts, pictographs—can be developed that can add life to a story?

Compete for control of visual messages. Do you have some strikingly colorful new product or company symbol that could excite the publication? You can ignore this opportunity. You can let the press rely on third-party services like Standard & Poor's, Dun & Bradstreet, Lipper Analytical, and the like. You can let the publication come up with its own graphics. Or, you can provide in-depth, specially designed graphic concepts that give the journalist an angle that "grabs." Which do you think has the best odds of putting across your story?

Watch out for the ginger ale. If your photograph will appear in a story, you need to think about how it's taken: Are you sitting? Are you standing? Who is in the photograph? Are you in shirt sleeves? Are charts and graphs going to be next to you? Do you have your coat on? Are you in the office? Is it windy? Is your hair blowing? Is there a cigarette on the table? For example, don't let yourself be photographed next to a glass of ginger ale and ice. Half of the people who see a color photo like that will conclude that it's a slug of bourbon. Each one of these touches can make a statement about you personally.

Think of yourself out of context. A photograph is indeed worth a thousand words . . . and there are a million things to think about when a photograph is taken. Who can forget the 1984 *Business Week* cover of Gulf Oil Chairman Jim Lee? Gulf had just been the victim of the largest corporate takeover to date. The title screamed out "Why Gulf Fell" in 100-point type, and there was Lee, holding his glasses with his hand shrouding his eyes and his brow furrowed. He looked forlorn. Undoubtedly, Lee had just taken his glasses off to rub his eyes during the interview or photo session, but what a wrong moment to rub his eyes.

If you are really shrewd, you can sometimes use the photo opportunity to your advantage. In 1989, *Business Week* did a profile of Chicago U.S. Attorney Anton Valukas. The article portrayed Valukas as a "grim-faced prosecutor [and] fraudbuster" who was cracking down on corruption and financial crime. The article notes that Valukas "declined to be interviewed" for the glowing—and, I might add, well-deserved—story. But, the photo of Valukas is something else. I would bet that while Valukas avoided the interview, he willingly posed for the photo. There he sits in his crisp white shirt: tough-jawed, straight-cuffed, set forward, in a pose that reminds you of Jack Webb, with a dreamily out-of-focus American eagle in the background. A real coup. But, this is risky business. When a photographer is in the room, think about your wedding pictures or your college yearbook. Your first objective is to be captured with dignity.

I recall once being in a group photo with Texas Senator Lloyd Bentsen. Bentsen ended up on the extreme right of this spontaneous photo opportunity. As the photographer lifted his camera, the senator suddenly clutched and shook my right hand. After the click, I blurted out, "Senator, I'm flattered." "Don't be, son," he smiled back, "I just wanted to make sure that they didn't crop me out of the photo."

23

Television and the Electronic Agenda

There are a number of good manuals to prepare a manager for appearing on television. Perhaps the best of them is Roger Ailes' book *You Are the Message* (Dow Jones-Irwin, 1987).

I want to emphasize six basics about television and the manager.

Television time is different from "real" time. A minute is an eternity. As Ailes says, "If you're just talking for 60 seconds, you'd better be good and interesting." Get your messages out quickly, in clear, simple terms.

Television viewers expect entertainment. You could be on a high-spirited talk show or introducing a training tape on capital investment. In either case, the audience still wants something extra. Any televised message needs life and color to reach its audience. Find ways to express yourself through memorable or amusing anecdotes or analogies. Even if your subject is grave, you have to hold people's attention. That's much tougher when you're on TV than when you are communicating in person.

Know your audience. Every television program has a target audience or range of audiences. Decide which part of the audience you want to reach and how you will convince them. Your concept of this audience has to be especially clear because you can't see them react.

Stay focused on your real audience. An interview is just a means to reach the broader audience. Your purpose for being there is not to talk to the interviewer. Don't allow yourself to be provoked or goaded or manipulated, by showing anger, for example, or in any way that would distort your message to your ultimate audience.

Respect the difference between live and taped television. If you agree to do a taped interview that can then be edited, you have just exposed yourself in a very dangerous way. Beware of the editor's knife. Decide in advance what your "must air" points are and stress them several times in a taped interview. Keep your points brief and make your point at the start of each sentence. Don't overexpose yourself: The reporter should be able to get everything he needs in 15 to 20 minutes of shooting. Be careful about when you breathe in an important sentence: Who knows which part of your thought might be asked to stand alone. Don't silently nod your head: God knows what you will later be seen agreeing to. Don't make controversial statements that can easily be lifted out of context. And, in either live or taped television, don't give a smile of understanding when another person is describing a misfortune.

Get media training. Media training is not a launch for an ego trip; it is self-defense, the martial arts of communication. No manager these days knows when he will end up in front of the klieg lights and the cameras because a pirate is gunning for his company or his plastics plant blows up. This isn't acting school. The media are a technology that you can either use or be used by. It's up to you.

———

There are countless other rules and tips that help managers come off well on television. But, these six should keep a manager on course. Dealing with the electronic media is a much more individual challenge than dealing with print journalism. So, seek the best possible media training. Of course, there's also no substitute for experience. In our era, that kind of experience and training should begin early in a manager's career.

Once a manager or a company is competent in dealing with television, the next step is to create one's own agenda for television. Here's how:

Exploit the dominance of business and economic news in broadcasting. We may look back at this point in time and call it the "era of broadcast and business news." Several months ago, NBC's John Chancellor told me that a change had been taking place in the broadcast agenda for foreign affairs. "For the foreseeable future," he said, "foreign affairs will be dominated by productivity and economic issues . . . more than war or revolution. The recent troubles in China, the Soviet Union, and Poland, for example, had more to do with economics than anything else." Chancellor is one of the most gifted on-air commentators. His views are also shared by the most forward-looking behind-the-scenes news managers, such as CBS News Vice-President Tom Bettag.

Bettag believes "the economy is the most important ongoing story in the news." He also says that television will have growing importance in transmitting economic and business information. "In any major economic crisis, only broadcast carries the news fast enough. The October 1987 market crash was a real eye-opener for the networks. I think all of us realized then that we had dramatically underestimated the importance of economic news." Increasingly, television news stories are about trade wars, embargoes, the spread of technology, and transnational takeovers.

Learn the tools of proactive video. As businesses themselves, broadcast operators today are aggressively cutting expenses, just as the demand for news programming (which is still the cheapest type to produce) grows. Firms and trade associations are filling the void with timely professionally produced information. More and more firms are putting out video news releases that package company messages used in local and network news programming.

Aspirin is declared to have significant new medical benefits in treating heart disease. Within hours of the announcement, an aspirin maker sends out a video news release, in this case actually beaming it through our satellite uplink, to hundreds of stations. The release doesn't mention our client's brand name, but it helps build awareness for the product category in an important new application. Companies donate sophisticated new equipment to help in a foreign disaster. The news release shows the equipment being loaded into cargo craft with the company name and logo visible. A fruit suspected of contamination is taken off the market. Sales sag. A video release now heralds the product's return with confidence-building endorsements from health authorities.

The video news release has such subtle power that information activists have been clamoring for Washington regulators to step in and control its use. Opponents want on-screen labeling of the information's source. I doubt this will happen since journalists themselves will police out the blatantly self-serving before it is aired. Instead, I expect the video news release medium to grow rapidly.

The video news release is just one of the new electronic tools of influence. We are constantly experimenting with the emerging technology in our firm. We are conducting more and more video news conferences—many of them global—that instantly bring together trade and financial audiences throughout the world.

A firm in Chicago has devised a shopping cart with a mini–TV screen. It receives narrowcasted advertising for a product while the consumer pushes the cart down the very aisle in which the product is displayed. Toys R Us and A&P now have their own radio networks that mix music programming for shoppers with ads for their respective stores. As you can see, there are a lot of ingenious ways to bust through the media clutter. But, you can only do it by knowing and mastering the media trends.

Weave your message into the new video fabric. *Sports Illustrated* put its twenty-fifth-anniversary swimsuit issue on videotape. Chrysler seized the opportunity. Not only do they have an advertising presence on the tape's cover but they also appear as a sponsor on the tape itself.

Organizations with a message are finding creative new ways to intrude in the program content itself. While viewers are zapping out commercials, they are hooked on talk, magazine, and information shows. The Nielsen and Arbitron rating services report that the average viewer watches four hours of such programming each week. Television execs know that this area is the fastest growing in TV programming. If you want to check out the trends in TV programming, the place to go is the annual convention of the National Association of Television Program Executives, where all syndicated programming is bought. For the past two years, all the action has been around information programming: Donahue, Oprah Winfrey, and others.

Reach your audience when they are naturally thinking about you. Gatorade was one example. Narrowcasting TV messages to shopping carts is another, and that's not some random gimmick. A research institute in 1986 found that two-thirds of all purchasing decisions are made in the store. The "woman of the household" is no longer lounging at home making decisions about drain cleaners between episodes of her soap operas. Effective marketing influence means reaching consumers at the most receptive moment. Gerber now pipes in videotapes on infant nutrition to captive audiences in hospital maternity wards. Can you imagine a concern more important to a new mother than the proper feeding of her baby? This kind of thinking has yielded Gerber a 73 percent market share for the baby food business in the United States.

Part VI

UNDERSTANDING THE GOVERNMENT AND THE SPECIAL INTERESTS

24

Playing the Iron Triangle

As with the media, you cannot influence government. Don't try. It will backfire. In the spring of 1989, Charles Black, a principal of Black, Manafort and Stone, boasted he peddled influence in the Department of Housing and Urban Development scandal.

Well, plenty of people are being prosecuted because they were involved in that scandal and many reputations were ruined. Those business leaders I know deplored Black's boast. Top people know that fairness must always find its way to the top in our pluralistic society. But while you can't and shouldn't try to influence government, the role influence plays in Washington is immense.

While American business exhibits a newfound appreciation for the importance of government, businesspeople, as individuals, still have many lessons to learn about Washington. Foremost is that the power in a business center such as New York City is very different from power in political capitals like Washington.

The great truth about power in Washington is that it is fleeting. In contrast, power in New York has more stamina because it is based on money. Power in Washington is rooted solely in "being in power." Former Secretary of State Cyrus Vance is a very bright man, but he has more influence with the media than in Washington today. If Clayton Yeutter had moved from U.S. trade representative to private citizen instead of agriculture secretary he would have lost more power than people realize, considerable power. In contrast, retired executives, individual entrepreneurs, and even heirs to great fortunes in business centers can have great power. They need only prove they remain connected to the power structure and the Favor Bank.

Hill and Knowlton's Washington office, headed by Bob Gray, is the largest lobbying organization in the world. It's situated in the Washington Harbour development near a building known both historically and affectionately as "The Power House." We represent companies of all sizes. Many smaller companies come to Hill and Knowlton because they want to have the contacts we can deliver. It's a way to ratchet themselves up. It gives them new status and a competitive edge. One high-tech company near San Francisco hired our Washington office simply to catch the eye of another high-tech company on the East Coast.

The successful businessperson in Washington will learn the rules and realities of how Washington works. Many managers believe a great deal of mythology about Washington and recent trends there. For example, many associate the Reagan years with cutbacks in the role of government, especially the federal government. Dr. Murray Weidenbaum, the head of the Council of Economic Advisors for part of the Reagan era, provides some interesting facts: "In 1981, the head count of federal civilian employees was 2.8 million. In 1986, the total exceeded 3.0 million"; ". . . Farm price supports, rose from $1 billion in 1976 to $12 billion in 1986"; "The budgets for members of the Senate and House, their staff[s], and their supporting agencies grew from $678 million in 1976 to $1.4 billion in 1986, a bit more than doubling . . ."

In short, the heralded Reagan years of "less government" did nothing at all to reduce the scale of federal government, and certainly the Reagan presidency did not preside over any reduction in expense. Weidenbaum has told me privately that the most important lesson to learn about power in Washington is that "the number of people involved in the process has expanded terrifically. Legislation has become a much smaller tail end in the process." The head count and budget changes mirror the new way government works. Weidenbaum added, "Congressional staffs have significantly expanded the power base of Congress and the media is serving as the transmission belt for the output of these staffs, special interests, and the think tanks."

The body count of congressional staffs has changed how Congress works. It has also expanded the power of even the most junior House member. Late in 1988, Business Roundtable Chairman and Pfizer CEO Edmund Pratt put his finger on the magnitude of change that has taken place. In a speech, he noted, "[House] Speaker Sam Rayburn was a member of Congress for *twelve years* before he gave his *first speech* in the House of Representatives. Today, a new congressman gets his own *subcommittee* in considerably less than half that time."

Perhaps the truest observation of the Reagan presidency was the comment President Reagan himself made shortly before his retirement, when he lashed out at "the iron triangle of the media, special interest groups, and parts of Congress." Understanding power in Washington means understanding the structure of Reagan's "iron triangle," and understanding, too, that the executive branch bureaucracy is largely a servant to those three forces.

There is no doubt that dealing with government is going to be an increasingly important part of a manager's job. The greater number of committees will seek to investigate more things. Investigative journalism will uncover a steady stream of issues that will increase the contact between regulators, elected officials, and businesspeople. Global competitive and trade issues will force business and government to work together more often and in a more detailed way. Managers will be called upon to show their skills in governmental affairs more often and earlier in their careers.

Dealing with national political figures, in Washington and the state capitals, I have found nine important keys to working the back halls of Washington. I call them the Beltway Rules of the Road:

Learn how people got where they are. The best way to gain access to a Washington cabinet member is to understand the political process that led to that cabinet member's appointment. Is the secretary there because his specialized knowledge is unrivaled, or because he is the conduit to the industrial leadership of the South, or because he is a key back-room strategist in designing the financing program for the next election? All of these considerations, and many others, can influence the appointment of a cabinet official or the selection of a candidate for any political office. If you understand these factors, you are much more likely to hit on an appeal that will set yourself apart from the other people who come pleading their causes or glad-handing into his office.

An easy way to learn about people's motives and power base is to monitor their social agenda. On any given night there are probably forty different social events in Washington. Power figures are very selective about which of these events they attend. If I want to know what Ways and Means Chairman Dan Rostenkowski's top agenda issues are, I'd learn those people, organizations, and interests whose functions Rostenkowski makes a point of attending.

Work through the staffs. Some top managers recoil at this, because they are hung up on the prestige of presenting their case only to people of the right rank. I'm afraid many of them go to Washington so that when they return to Fargo or Beaumont they can boast that they just met with the secretary of the treasury or the attorney general. The astute businesspeople, the ones who "get the cakes baked," know that's not enough. After you or your boss makes the symbolic contact at the top, you should follow up personally with the key staff people. A cabinet secretary can be effective, powerful, and committed to help you, but there are tens of thousands of people on his payroll, many of them lifers from the Civil Service bureaucracy. If they decide in Wichita that they aren't going to do it, it won't happen. And so it goes in every federal agency. You need to know the senior staff people who control the action in the field and in the bureaucracy.

Know the experts. There are true experts on individual issues in Washington and the state capitals. Don't fool around with a general lobby. Go to the experts. Charls Walker pretty much wrote the tax code in Washington. If you want to make a change in the tax code, you go to him. In Pennsylvania, a lawyer named Dave Dunlap wrote the Public Utility Holding Act. He knows it cold, every little nuance, every comma. In each state and throughout Washington, there are people like that. Forget the back-slappers and the name-droppers. Go to the people who have the substantive knowledge.

Learn the ropes of Washington testimony. I know managers who lunge at the opportunity to give testimony in Washington. The overriding question I always pose when that "opportunity" comes up is "Why do it?" Frankly, why not leave it to your trade association or to your competitors? If you testify, you better have clear purposes both for you and your firm. On a slow news day in summer, you can suddenly find yourself sweating in front of the Washington cameras and on the evening news, having plunged yourself into some controversy you never dreamed of. When Mr. Smith goes to Washington these days, he better be damn careful of how he's exposing himself.

We regularly set up mock hearings for people to train them before they testify. We re-create the hearing room and even put photographs of senators and representatives on the chairs. We also brief people on the staff behind the senator or congressman. We train clients to anticipate the style as well as the substance of a congressional grilling.

You may get only five minutes in Washington. You may be scheduled at the end of the day. That five minutes can make or break you. You have to treat it the same way you treat the sound byte or the news interview. Watch out if a committee puts you on its agenda late in the day. That's not just because the committee will be tired and edgy. They could be nailing the window shut on your side of the story.

You may not see or hear what an investigator turns up today, this month, or even this year. But you can be sure you will hear about it at some future date. There are individuals and committees collecting storehouses of information about your company and maybe even you personally. At some point, that will be dragged out. Congressman Neal Smith made a career of "creaming" Iowa Beef over alleged transgressions that had been committed twenty years ago.

The CEO of Iowa Beef was to testify in some "rerun" hearings dealing with meat products in Washington. Year after year, Smith kept bringing the CEO back to work him over on the same old story. Whenever the CEO was brought in to testify, he would end up in the 4:45 testimony slot. Each time he appeared, Iowa Beef got plastered in a newspaper headline or a TV story. Smith always finished just in time to put across his position, but Iowa Beef never had the chance to rebut.

The TV shows were all blocked out; the papers were all wrapped; the writers were all back in their offices at their typewriters. So, we finally just broke complete stories in *advance* of the committee meetings because the committee was playing dirty pool with the company. It helped balance the stories and brought an end to the scheduling games.

Watch bellwether states for the national legislative agenda.
Although Washington bureaucracy has grown, Washington's
role as the source of legislative initiatives has diminished.
During the Reagan presidency, not a single new piece of
national regulatory legislation was enacted. *Industry Week* reports that every year, between 150,000 and 200,000 bills are
introduced in state legislatures. That's twice as many as a
decade ago. Between 30,000 and 40,000 become law. The
vast majority of new job openings in lobbying are at the state,
not the national, level.

Certain key states, such as California, Massachusetts, Michigan, Florida, and Texas, will pass legislation on insurance or day
care, and the trend is for such legislation to be "carbon copied,"
often in ten to twenty states in a matter of months. Smart
companies and managers are monitoring these trend-setting
states for legislation that may have implications for them. More
time is being spent by companies in such states, with the
awareness that these state capitals are really the back door
to national policy. The insurance industry, as one example,
spent more than $40 million on influence campaigns sur-
rounding 1988 referendums and initiatives *in California alone.*

**Structure every appeal to a congressman in terms of his
constituency.** Let's say that you must deal with a congressman
who has every ideological reason to oppose you on a certain
issue. The past evidence—his voting record, his speeches,
his key financial backers—all say he will be against you. The
best way to attack the problem is to show how his constituency
is going to lose if it opposes you. That loss may be jobs, foreign
investment, private charitable contributions, whatever. You
should make it very clear to the congressman that you will also
be pointing out these potential losses to his constituency.

Know that government is always the lead story in Washington.
I had our research department go back to examine the pe-

riod between February 1 and March 1, 1989, not known to be a dramatic period in international affairs. During that time, the city of Washington had terrible experiences involving its mayor, drugs, and murders, to name just the lowlights. Despite these problems, the lead story in the *Washington Post* was a national political story every day. In effect, the *Post* is the trade paper of Washington politics.

A businessperson working with the Washington press should expect to have his story understood in terms of government impact. The readership and viewership inside the Beltway see life mainly from this slant, so that's how the media pitches the news. To an extent, things are changing today, as Washington is developing into a regional business hub, but the overwhelming center of gravity remains government.

Be a source of intelligence or connections. Bringing information or intelligence is one way to ingratiate yourself to either an elected or an appointed government official. Maybe it's bringing inside news or "intellectual capital" in the form of new insights from your planning or research staff. Industry sources developed material that was used by Bush, Dukakis, and many members of Congress in the most recent national campaign. Business organizations and individuals wrote speeches, developed ads, and did whatever had to get done. Dick Gephardt's data on trade didn't just come from his staff; it came from firms and unions with very specific interests.

You also may be able to market yourself as a "back-channel bridge." Often, there are no lines of communication from one person or camp to another. Because of entrenched positions or lack of personal contacts, the one can't or doesn't talk with the other. "Backchannelers" bridge that gap. Retired executives, trade association heads, and the clergy are good backchannelers. The press and politicians are often *not* good at this. (They tend to leak things that end up on the news.) You can be very useful to a government official if you can bridge special interests that the official can't afford to deal with or can't succeed in dealing with. Maybe you have a route to the Nature Conservancy or the Urban League or the National Rifle Association. Armand Hammer of Occidental Petroleum has long been an informal channel of communication with the Kremlin. So is Dwayne Andreas of ADM. Chuck Percy is tight with India. Dick Allen is very close to Korea. Felix Rohatyn has good contacts with both France and South America.

Don't expect government to have an affectionate relationship with business. Felix Rohatyn, who really came to understand the nature of business-government cooperation in his work bailing out New York City, once said to me, "In general, business-government partnerships are a misnomer. Business can be helpful in a particular crisis or emergency. Over time, they are rarely in sync. Their relationships are too adversarial."

Frank Silbey is now a private consultant. For years, he did investigative work for some of the most powerful congressional oversight committees. Silbey believes that most of Washington is simply contemptuous of business. "Washington thinks of business," he once said to me, "as so much meat on the hoof."

25

The General Rules of Special Interests

Special interests continue to multiply. They are shrewder and more manipulative communicators than you can imagine. They can quickly cut a company's legs out from under it. We often advise client companies on how to deal with special interests. Sometimes the key role we play is educative. It's surprising how few managers recognize the long-term power of such groups as the Rainbow Coalition. They also don't see other trends. For example, ethnic blocks—African-American, Polish, Jewish—are becoming very powerful once again. That's because our society is fragmenting, and people want a greater sense of identity.

Another reason special interests spring up so rapidly is that most of the mainstream institutions in our society have lost their voice. The academic community has become so technical that it speaks only to itself. Religion and government have been discredited by a seemingly endless series of scandals, which is forcing people to rally around more tightly defined causes such as animal rights or aid for the homeless elderly. The special-interest advocate of the 1970s would look like a general do-gooder compared with today's sharply identified special-interest leader.

The process for advocating special interests has become much more systematic. When you see a book on a cause, such as abortion or tort reform or the decay of our highway infrastructure, it's usually safe to assume that some specific interest—profit or nonprofit—is backing its writing. There are some 5,000 nongovernmental organizations in the world that marshal the forces of special interests. From pamphleteering to direct mail to telephone campaigns and task force mobilization, some of the best marketing I have ever seen is conducted by special interests. The tool that has empowered special interests most is television, because television can be emotionally compelling and can turn up the volume of any individual's or small group's complaint very effectively. In the modern age, television appeals are the backbone of any special-interest group.

Few businesses know how to advance their interests with the same skill that nonbusiness special interests do. Businesses, especially in the United States, are so busy being competitive with each other that they don't know how to coalesce well on common causes. The American Petroleum Institute and the American Retail Federation are two of the few effective business lobbies because they doggedly and tightly go after a limited number of issues. Volatile special-interest confrontations can arise with astonishing suddenness. Today's manager is likely to encounter special interests both inside and outside the organization, and is well advised to study the principles of negotiating with special interests.

Learn how to horse trade. You can't make it seem that way, but dealing with special interests is purely and simply horse trading. Even if the special-interest cause is intensely humanistic, you can expect any effective interest group leader to deal like a riverboat gambler. Gandhi is a terrific example: He knew that his odds of getting rid of the British were much higher through passive resistance than armed rebellion. Badly trained and ill-equipped Indian nationals would have had a rough time beating the British army. But, Gandhi knew that the idea of rolling British tanks over passive demonstrators or bayoneting the defenseless would be too humiliating for British morality. Gandhi's passivity banged the British over the head. He knew how to horse trade with the British, and I'm sure he was smart enough to know that the same tactic would have failed against Ayatollah Khomeini or Che Guevara.

Gorbachev and Lech Walesa are doing this horse trading. They have discovered a mutuality of purpose: the pursuit of hard currency for Poland. So, Poland gets a generous grant from the Bush administration, and Walesa makes his first U.S. trip to address the AFL-CIO and the United States Congress. Other masters of the art of horse trading are the UAW, the Urban League, and the Southern Christian Leadership Conference.

Find out what gives the special interest credibility. Crain's *City & State* publisher Dan Miller once described to me the evolution that has taken place in economic special interests. In earlier times, business development in a certain city sector would have been represented by some arm of the local Chamber of Commerce, and no one would take it seriously, Dan contends. Now there are neighborhood business development groups that have a clear agenda and actively lobby the press. Their credibility often comes from the tight definition of the group itself. Neighborhood groups have power. The neighborhood is tangible. Vague national organizations have weak identities. For years, Adam Clayton Powell's congressional district in Harlem had a more powerful voice for the black community than many national black organizations.

Identify the specific issue and demands. Too often, businesses will get a demand from a special-interest group and react to the group's ideology or ethnic background. It's true that the group's demands are usually part of a broader cause or agenda, but that is largely irrelevant. The immediate job is to quickly get a handle on the issue at stake and what is wanted in particular.

Settle a problem with a special-interest group before it goes public. Don't wait until people are picketing your factory to settle an issue with a special-interest group. Once the pickets are up, or they are boycotting your store, the special interest has enlisted its most powerful potential ally, the media. Those companies that do the most effective job of handling special interests always make sure that they have an open line of communication to their worst adversaries. With the exception of some wild-eyed idealists, most don't really get any pleasure out of riots or demonstrations. The smartest special interests deal with the sharpest big businesses through the process of constant and quiet underground horse trading. You rarely hear about red-lining disputes or class-action discrimination with big companies today. But, those very topics and countless others are talked about quietly every day. Special interests and big companies have continuous, low-key discussions through forums like Chicago United, Detroit Renaissance, the North Texas Commission, and Forward Atlanta.

Always calculate your concessions in advance and then figure out how not to give them up. The worst mistake companies make is to go into the negotiation figuring that they will give up nothing . . . and then be negotiated into giving up more than they really had to. Calculate each level of concession in advance and the degree of conciliation you expect for it.

Pocket your cherries. I learned a very important lesson on bargaining from the UAW's Doug Fraser in a late-night session at the Palmer House in Chicago. We were sitting

230

around talking, eating stale sandwiches and drinking sodas, and Fraser said, "Look, before you go into any bargaining session, have three or four cherries in your pocket. Don't bring them out until you are absolutely ready to use them. These are giveaway things. Here's what I am going to give you; now I need a concession back from you. These things deal with that person's point of view." Don't use blood-and-marrow issues to soften the opposition. Let's say that you're a drug-store chain. Senior citizens are picketing you over your prescription-pricing policies. To hype sales midweek, you have long been considering a 10 percent discount for seniors on all store merchandise. During the negotiations, you reach into your pocket and toss their cherry on the table. It could defuse the entire confrontation.

Use neutral avenues such as the arts to get to special interests. The arts, at least usually, are neutral. The board committees of arts organizations mix together business leaders with the most prominent social activists and community leaders. I know of one large city where the symphony committee for young people's concerts brought together a prominent manufacturer and a leading housing activist. During one very hot summer that social bond and the contact it provided did a better job of preventing a race riot than any official channel did.

Don't try to eradicate a special interest. Assume the special interest is never going to go away. It's like an infection that resides permanently in the body. You may resolve the redlining issue in one region in the United States, but it's going to come back. You may eradicate drug abuse in Oregon only to have it erupt in Georgia. You may take ground on tort reform in California only to lose turf in Massachusetts. One reason why special interests never disappear—and I say this as a realist, not a cynic—is that any special interest is self-perpetuating. First, there is a cadre of volunteers whose celebrity is based on the interest's staying alive. Second, any large movement has a staff of administrators and bureaucrats whose livelihood rests on stringing the issue out or evolving it into a newer, sexier one.

Identify and disarm the rallying points of the group. Force the discussion to become more specific. Generalizations and emotional appeals are the heart of special-interest-group tactics. Look at the evidence you have available to you. As you focus the discussion, how can you counteract each of the allegations with evidence presented in an emotionally compelling way? Anticipation is the best weapon and counteraction remains the best strategy. Look for every opportunity to refute what your adversary is saying, both about your style and your actual actions and policies.

If an animal rights group talks about the cruelty of experiments to animals, you counter with the cruelty of needless suffering by human cancer patients because the lack of animal subjects slows down research. If a wealthy neighborhood group opposes designating a local street as a truck route, you point out that a new plant in the community needs that route. Without it, the plant won't be built, the community will lose hundreds of potential jobs, and the city's poor will be hurt worst of all.

Watch for group splintering. Solidarity between minority groups, for example, is on the decline. There is growing friction between black and Puerto Rican Americans. Mexican auto workers who belong to the UAW in Detroit have accelerating rivalries with Mexican auto workers working in *maquiladora* assembly plants across the border from San Antonio. You must also look at special interests in a broad context: not just what they stand for but what conflicts or potential conflicts they create. Up until the 1970s, conservationists and environmentalists usually shared the same agenda. In the western United States today, there are sharp differences between conservationists and environmentalists. When any special interest becomes large enough, it invariably begins to fragment.

For each particular controversy, assign one person and hold that person accountable. Nothing enhances the case for any special-interest group more than to find their targeted villain issuing conflicting and contradictory statements. If the controversy is a heated one, you can also assume that the character of the battlefield will shift daily and perhaps hourly. Such a situation can only be effectively managed with one person at the helm—and that person better have the rank, authority, and communications skill to be credible and persuasive.

Be aware that winning has risks, too. The greatest risk is that you will make the interest a martyr, if your victory is draconian and decisive. Abolishing a special interest is the kind of Spartacus story that the national investigative media just love. There is a good argument for keeping the interest alive but anemic. The IBEW—the International Brotherhood of Electrical Workers—is a "sweetheart union." There have been very few disruptions in power plants for as long as I can remember. In certain industries, management will favor the continuing existence of a less aggressive union to keep a stronger union out.

Study counterculture methods. Businesses would be much further ahead if they studied the tactics used by nonprofit interest groups. The *Wall Street Journal*, not long ago, described a new twist in public protests called "tag-team fasting." The *Journal* reporter chronicled how Cesar Chavez, Jesse Jackson, and actor Martin Sheen spent successive time in "the fast lane" protesting the use of pesticides on grapes.

This "relay" fasting, often of a day or two, was "sort of a bucket brigade with a bare bowl." But the changing cast of characters kept the issue alive for weeks.

I'm close to those people who play major roles in our nation's policy agendas, but I have rarely if ever seen our nation's leadership map out a program that would sustain attention on an issue. Let's say the topic is technical education: Why shouldn't twenty top CEOs caucus and pledge to surrender one of their major annual speaking engagements to the issue of technical education, each speech endorsing just the same four key points? A clear message could travel from Town Hall in Los Angeles to the Economic Club in Detroit to the hearing chambers on Capitol Hill. The program could be reinforced with video news releases and targeted mailings and reach a crescendo on a Hollywood sound stage or the steps of the White House. We think of orchestrating the Olympics that way and presidential elections are certainly won with those methods, but rarely does business collaborate on essential common issues with that kind of multidimensional thinking.

Learn how the think tanks work. Business spends more than $800 million a year funding research in universities. Almost all of it is technological or scientific. The biggest single recipient is Massachusetts Institute of Technology, which gets roughly $35 million a year in business grants. Yet business is unsuccessful in getting ideological support from universities. Why? Professors today are so specialized that no one understands them. Where universities have stopped, private think tanks have taken over. Think tanks are replacing universities as the intellectual power centers of business. The American Enterprise Institute, the Cato Institute, and the Hudson Institute are three of the power think tanks. At the think tanks, scholars and business leaders study problems and devise solutions, which means they take positions. In this sense, think tanks are also displacing trade associations in developing the persuasive arguments needed by business.

Bill Hammett, president of another think tank, the prestigious Manhattan Institute, believes think tanks have a very pragmatic role. He says, "Leaders in business and government must devise new ways of understanding and explaining what's going on in their fields. What we need most today is bold vision, relevant information, and straightforward logic." As one example, the Manhattan Institute has a four-year plan to renovate public education in New York City and to make it a model for national educational reform.

Think tanks are business' way of making a substantive contribution to the public policy agenda. Think tanks have taken over the job of mobilizing press and opinion leader views. The best think tanks are committed to challenging simplistic biases. For example, one recent paper attacked the notion that tort and liability reform is simply the battle between greedy doctors versus greedy lawyers versus greedy insurance companies egged on by even greedier publicists and politicians. Professor Klaus Schwab, president of the World Economic Forum which is the organizer of the prestigious Davos Symposium in Switzerland, believes in a strong action bias for think tanks. In the case of Davos, only government, academic, and business officials actively in power can participate. But, that can yield results in lightning speed. Such was the case early in 1988 when a Davos meeting forged a breakthrough in Turkish/Greek relations, which had been stalled for decades, and set a number of potent economic initiatives into motion.

———

Dealing with environmentalists is a particularly tricky issue for businesspeople. What makes the problem so complex is the active role the press takes in reporting on environmental issues. If you look at most business-environmentalist clashes, a company's effectiveness in explaining risk to the press almost always determines the outcome.

There are already very strong environmental laws on the books. In the past several years, business has benefited from lax enforcement, which is ending, and Title III hazardous waste reporting is the beginning of that end. A more moderate executive branch, a shift toward re-regulation, and a stronger Congress will amplify this trend. The Bush administration has signaled that it will have a much tougher environmental agenda than the Reagan administration. Five decisive issues will dominate the environmental agenda in the foreseeable future: acid rain, the globalization of environmental problems, modifying nature through genetic engineering and chemicals, waste management, and the changing methods of environmental activists.

Rutgers University Professor Peter Sandman is the leading expert on explaining environmental issues to the press. Many of the following tactics are adaptations from an Environmental Protection Agency pamphlet by Professor Sandman. It is quite probably the best document ever written on communicating about environmental issues.

Speak to the hazards that exist. Journalists focus on one issue in covering environmental stories. The journalists' job is to establish if a hazard exists and what will be done about it. After risk is established, they have little interest in the scientific background. They want to know who caused it and what will be done about it.

Hammer home clear, straightforward messages. Reporters cover viewpoints, not truths. They are neither interested in extreme positions nor those straight down the middle of the road. They want alternate paragraphs, spotlighting credible experts who debate that something is or is not a serious risk.

Reporters want to pin people down, so it's important for you to emphasize your key message again and again, and not waver from it.

Offer authoritative reassurance. Claims of risk are more newsworthy than claims of safety. Reporters will dramatize risk by making the language simpler and less technical. However, most articles about an environmental crisis are fundamentally reassuring rather than inflammatory. Recognize that the press welcomes statements of reassurance from an authoritative source, even though the news value is in the crisis. Reassurance will be best received if the positive statements are in clear, simple language.

Never tell a journalist that a health or safety risk is acceptable. Journalists and public officials don't believe in the concept of "acceptable risk." Steering clear of "acceptable risk" is one of the most difficult adjustments a businessperson must make in dealing with a journalist or a governmental official. Frank Mankiewicz, Robert Kennedy's communications advisor and a keen observer of the Washington scene, believes that a basic intolerance remains in Washington for "economic rationalizations"—that a problem is too expensive to fix. "If it's dangerous and you caused it, you fix it!" is the attitude. Of course, attitudes are malleable, but you better realize that this view is the first you are likely to encounter. It's the one you *have to* address.

Deal affected parties into the solution. People who feel wronged by an environmental problem will not accept any resolution—no matter how just—until they believe they share control of the solution. Countless case studies of negotiations have shown that once the "wronged" party feels that it shares control, it will spring into action at once, helping to think up creative solutions or compromises.

Get it out fast. In any environmental problem, a company or an agency is better off dealing with the public as soon as possible after it concludes that a problem exists. "An organization," Sandman writes, "is better off explaining why it doesn't yet have all the answers, than explaining why it didn't share them years ago."

Don't approach the public with jargon about probability. The scientist's explanation of risk will frustrate the public. The people best qualified to explain risk—scientists and technocrats—are often poor communicators. Many evidence two traits: overcommunication and lack of passion. Experts are famous for their conviction that no information may be left out. As the saying goes, "Unable to tell all, they often wind up telling nothing." And they ignore natural and legitimate emotions. These people are professionally disciplined to ignore feelings. How do people respond when their feelings are ignored? Sandman says, "They escalate—yell louder, cry harder, listen less—which in turn stiffens the experts." Technical people who must meet the press and public are key candidates for media training.

26

Labor Today

Unions are no longer run by Joe Lunchbucket. And they are making increasingly sophisticated demands. In 1986, Lynn Williams, who heads the United Steelworkers, proclaimed a formula that each dollar of "worker sacrifice" was to be redeemed with a dollar of profit sharing or stock. When he went against Wheeling-Pittsburgh Steel, Williams brought in investment banker Lazard Freres and accountant Arthur Young to help mold the strategy. The tactics in labor relations have come a long way.

Study the new style of union communication. Too few managers read union publications. Page through such journals as the UAW's *Skill* or *Solidarity* these days, and you will find articles on:

Global training with U.S. workers apprenticing on automated assembly equipment in Augsburg, Germany

How the unions are pressing for a "people-centered" approach to new technology introductions

How unions are encouraging women to enter the skilled trades

The appeals unions are shaping to attract the under-thirty worker

How organizers are targeting corporate greed as an explanation for management policy

Pictographs showing job-creation rates during Democratic versus Republican administrations

Each theme is treated in a way rank-and-file workers can understand. Each paints a "villain" that workers accept as credible, doing so more vividly than most company house organs would ever attempt. Not only is union communication more issue-focused today but it is written with the journalistic color and punch you would associate with Geraldo Rivera or *USA Today*.

Anticipate great subtlety in labor approaches. The relative scarcity of strikes in recent years is lulling management to sleep. Today's labor reprisal strategies are much subtler. The old picket line/lockout seesaw is as primitive as infantry lining up to shoot at each other. According to the *Wall Street Journal*, the AFL-CIO has distributed a book called *The Inside Game: Winning with Workplace Strategies*. In it, such tactics as filing mass grievances and staging production slowdowns are suggested. Unions have learned to hang on to their paychecks while they deprive management of much-treasured productivity. They are abandoning ham-fisted walkouts. Unions have evolved from being street-smart to being "suite-smart."

Strengthen the communications skills of first-level supervisors. To bolster competitiveness, companies have pushed for more productivity, and now labor is eager to push back. So, today's manager better be carefully tuned-in to the new methods. Smart companies know that the most influential force in worker-management relations is the first-level supervisor. Obviously, the communications skills of these people have a material effect on the real productivity of the company.

Expect women to be the new power in the labor movement.
Mature women in their thirties and forties will be very important to tomorrow's labor movement. These women defined themselves in the sixties, made a lot of progress in the
seventies, and then ran into a stone wall in the eighties.
Women make up 2 percent of the Senate, 6 percent of the
House, and 52 percent of the population. It doesn't add up.
Only 17 percent of U.S. workers are unionized. Two-thirds
of the new entrants to the work force are women. Plenty of
them are working mothers, strong backers of such social
programs as day care. Expect women, particularly those in
the service and information economy, to be the catalyst and
the leadership of the labor movement in the 1990s.

**Anticipate a more active voice from labor on ownership and
operation.** Charlie Bryan's mechanics' union almost ousted
Frank Lorenzo from control of Eastern Airlines in the 1989
Eastern strike and the subsequent negotiations to sell the
airline to Peter Ueberroth. We don't yet have co-determination,
worker membership on boards, the way they do in Europe.
Lee Iacocca shrewdly put the UAW's Doug Fraser on the
Chrysler board because he needed union help to turn Chrysler
around.

Employee stock ownership has introduced a new level of
accountability to workers. Goodly chunks of both J. C. Penney
and Procter & Gamble are owned by employees. Many employees are important stockholders and they take their ownership seriously. In some cases, the employees will just buy
the company, which is what happened to Avis.

Use employees to fight takeovers. Employees can be a potent
anti-takeover force. Most know that an unfriendly acquisition
can lead to a tremendous loss of jobs. If you want employees
on your side of a takeover, you're best off getting them there
long before a threat emerges. Don't count on making friends

on the shop floor when the pirates are banging on the door. Always have the employee audience in mind when you plan your total defense strategy. For example, the company spokesperson in a takeover crisis better be someone who has chalked up high marks for credibility with the workers.

Court retired employees. Management is finding that the employee population doesn't just include active workers. The guys and gals with the gold watches have also got the gold, which will be a factor in unexpected ways. The trend toward senior economic activism is on a sharp upswing. Retirees will be a bigger voice and are already important in takeover battles.

I remember attending a utility's stockholder meeting in the Southeast not long ago at which management proposed cutting the dividend. The proposal was greeted with boos, hisses, yells, and foot stomping. Who was raising the ruckus? A pack of money-hungry arbs, or a gang of Young Turks from Wall Street? Not on your life! They were all retirees— many former employees. Of all the hostile audiences you can encounter at an annual meeting, the one you least want to tangle with is a retiree group.

Conclusion

Long before I even heard of public relations, much less Hill and Knowlton, I had a job in a filling station. It was a Sohio station back in Columbus, and I was in high school.

A man brought in his car and said he wanted us to "check everything" because he was going to drive his family cross-country. I put the car up on the rack and did what I thought was a very thorough job; I checked his brakes, his tires, the fittings—everything. When I was finished I took it down from the hoist, drove it over to the wall, and parked it.

Just then Doug Rader, the station manager, came by and asked me if I had checked the car. I said yes.

"Bob," he said in an accusatory tone, "you only had it on the rack twenty minutes."

"I checked *everything*," I insisted.

"Do you realize," he said, fixing me with a cold eye, "it takes three to four *hours* to check a car the way that man wants his car checked? He's going to be driving his *family*, his wife and three kids, all the way across the country, and if anything goes wrong because you didn't check it, then you're responsible for what happens to those people."

Whew. Talk about guilt feelings. Doug Rader's brief lecture gave me an instant insight into the importance of two elements that I would later learn are essential in any business: quality and accountability.

I put that car back up on the rack and checked it out for *four hours*. You name it and I tightened it, lubricated it, or adjusted it until my hands and arms were numb. When the man came to pick up the car, he had no idea how hard I'd worked. But that didn't matter because *I* knew it. He could drive his family cross-country and back several times over before I'd have to worry about their safety. I'd given *quality* service and was fully accountable.

Quality and accountability. It may sound chauvinistic, but I like to think of those "virtues" as being traditionally American. I know they are a large part of the reason why I find it so satisfying to work in public relations and for Hill and Knowlton.

In the past quarter-century, I've had a lot of chances to leave Hill and Knowlton if I were so inclined. But hardly any of them interested me to the point of even thinking about it. What I so liked about my job was that the company gave me the opportunity to "do my own thing," but within a comfortable structure. And that too reminds me of America.

I once heard Irving Kristol, the scholar and teacher, say that democracy does not guarantee equality of conditions, it only guarantees equality of *opportunity*. Given my experience, I'd have to agree with that.

At the risk of sounding harsh, I'd have to say that for those who want to excel, there is no dole and no safety net. Democracy does not take the hard edge off the battles that each one of us must fight if he or she wants the distinction of success. And in fighting those battles and trying to earn the right to lead, businesspeople of today must operate from a thoughtful personal agenda that includes concern for others. Quality and accountability again, and intelligent use of the Power Triangle discussed at the book's beginning.

They must do *worthy* things, communicate sound messages, and seek recognition *quietly*. If pressed, I'd say that's my simple credo for making it in a very complicated world.

244

CONCLUSION

And as complicated as that world is, look at how quickly and deeply and, in some cases, fundamentally it is *changing*. Consider the convergence of certain events—all of which happened relatively recently—each one of which in its own special arena represents a sea change.

Nissan's contest with UAW said something very meaningful for labor, as did the RJR-Nabisco deal in the field of finance. In international finance it was Jimmy Goldsmith's offer for B.A.T., which meant that the "M&A" game (mergers and acquisitions) has moved into the international arena. In the environment, it was—hands down—the Exxon Valdez spill. In politics it was Jim Wright and Tony Coelho, and also Barney Frank, and in government the HUD scandal. As for the rest of American society, it's the surge in cocaine and crack use and abuse.

Also, over the last year the Japanese have shifted the game and are now going to play it on the field of quality, not just price. In what used to be called the Communist *bloc*, one hesitates to say what's happening without checking the day's news reports. To our north, the U.S.-Canadian Free Trade Pact has broken down that border, and a North American Trade Alliance seems to be coming together, while Argentina, Brazil, Venezuela, and Mexico attempt to do the same thing in Latin America.

In the Third World, the news is not so positive. I am very much afraid that in the near future the Third World is going to become the Fourth World. It is going to be relegated to the ash heap of history—those countries are going to get spent nuclear and chemical waste, and their people are going to be besieged like never before. To make matters even worse, they won't have any money. This will, I believe, cause big problems by the end of the 1990s.

Those are some of the pluses and minuses that will result from these "sea changes" in various areas of national and international life. But I have no intention of ending on a negative note. I did not go through this process simply so I could sound warnings. I feel far too upbeat about too many things taking place here and abroad for that.

Allow me to return to why I wanted to write this book in the first place. I'm not kidding when I say that I love this business of public relations, this *profession* of public relations (and I do consider it to be a profession). But I'm well aware that quite a few people view it with ambivalence and suspicion, and in a few rare cases outright hostility.

I can understand these impressions. For too long public relations has been shrouded in shadow and secrecy, green dust and black books, and the ever-popular blue smoke and mirrors. Certain practitioners have suggested they can control our lives through professional secrets. Don't you believe them.

The essence of public relations is the power of influence, and, as I hope I have made clear, that rests on a three-column base of quality, accountability, and . . . common sense (or "truth," if you want a more lofty synonym).

There are many very simple things people can easily learn that will help them advance their careers, help their companies prosper, or advance whatever cause they happen to be involved in, and I hope the preceding pages have made clear that there's nothing mystical or magical about the process. I've tried to bring in some light so you can see that there is no real mystery surrounding the proper use of influence.

I guess there's another reason I wrote this book—I love this business. Years ago, we had a CEO at Hill and Knowlton who used to say, and he said it only half-jokingly, "Anybody who takes a vacation is a Communist!" Now even *I* will admit that view is a bit extreme. I take vacations quite often, and I enjoy them thoroughly, but I will confess that when they're almost over I begin to feel a rising excitement, an anxiousness to get back to work on a job that for me has never ceased to be fun.

CONCLUSION

You don't believe me? Let me tell you about a job I just turned down. It was a most attractive job, one with a much higher profile than CEO of Hill and Knowlton, great challenges to do both well and good, and a salary that was not just a princely but a kingly sum.

This is what happened. Last May, I was at the St. Louis airport changing planes when I heard myself being paged. I went to the counter and learned I had a long-distance phone call. When I picked up the phone and heard the voice of Gerry Roche, my mind went on full alert. Anytime you get a call from Gerry Roche, of the executive search firm of Heidrick & Struggles, you know there's serious, *heavy* business involved. When it comes to head-hunting, Gerry is the pro's pro.

"Bob," he said, without any preamble, "I don't want you to go 'ballistic,' but I've recommended you to become the next commissioner of the National Football League."

I almost dropped the phone. I knew Pete Rozelle had indicated a desire to retire, and I had done some work over the years for the NFL and knew many of the owners, but I never put those two facts together and made them spell a job opportunity for *me.*

I was stunned to get the call. But then I started thinking about what that job could mean. The NFL commissioner, it seemed to me, could make a major impact on our national life in several areas. One, he could make a real impact on the drug problem in the United States by getting the League out front in the fight against drugs. The hero worship that so many kids give the players could be utilized in getting the anti-drug message across. Two, I thought that the job offered a chance to do something about the "under-education" of so many of the players in the League.

So, finding myself intrigued, I began what turned into a series of meetings with a number of the owners—Dan Rooney of the Pittsburgh Steelers, Wellington Mara of the New York

Giants, Lamar Hunt of the Kansas City Chiefs, Art Modell of the Cleveland Browns, and a whole host of others.

Just as one might imagine, the first meeting, which was to be held at the posh Regency Hotel in Manhattan, took place with a certain amount of flair—and great secrecy. I was instructed to call the room of Wellington Mara, which I did, whereupon I was told he was not registered. Nor, I found out next, was Lamar Hunt.

Puzzled, I was debating what to do next when I saw Lamar Hunt, whom I had never met but knew from newspaper and magazine photos, coming toward me. Putting his fingers to his lips, he whispered, "Let's go quickly," and guided me wordlessly into a vacant elevator. The owners did not want any of the "candidates" to see one another.

(Interestingly, throughout the process of selection, the press always had the NFL search wrong. They were constantly bringing up the names of people the owners were not considering. What was happening was that a number of high-level people were trying to manipulate the press in order to invent their own candidacy for the job. Again, it reminded me that very often one has to take what one reads in the press with a grain of salt.)

In my meetings with the owners, I made it clear that if I took the job my priorities would be the drug issue and the education issue, and after that the question of how to negotiate the best television contract or what to do about the prospect of playing League games in Europe, for example. The owners, as it turned out, saw things just the other way around, and once I realized that, I began to disengage myself from the selection process.

I don't mean to suggest, by the way, that the owners were not forthright or decent in their dealings with me. They were. In fact, they could not have been better. A prime example of this would be my salary "demands." Even though I had told them up front that it would take a lot of money for me to "jump" from Hill and Knowlton to the League, I am not sure they expected me to ask for quite as much as I did. Yet when I told them it would take a healthy seven figures—a year, for five years—they didn't even blink when they said yes.

In looking back to see why I decided against taking the job, one point stands out that may be significant. From the very beginning of the negotiations, I insisted that my name be kept out of the press. I did this because I didn't want my Hill and Knowlton clients to read my name in the press and think that they would not be getting my full attention and effort as the selection process ground on. But in retrospect I think that maybe the reason I was so insistent was that I knew in the back of my mind that I was never *really* going to leave Hill and Knowlton and public relations.

In any event, I was thrilled to have been considered, and I wish Paul Tagilabue, the new commissioner, all the best.

Only one thing worries me about this whole NFL affair: What in the world am I going to say when Geoffrey, my sports-mad four-year-old son, becomes old enough to read this book, and discovers what I've declined? I can just hear him now: "You mean you could have been the commissioner of the *National Football League*, and you turned it down to stay in *public relations!!?!!*"

I guess then will be the time to give him my lecture about the importance of quality and accountability, and to let him in on a little secret. The main difference between the job I turned down and the job I kept is that in comparison with the NFL commissioner, the CEO of Hill and Knowlton has a lot more . . . *influence.*

Notes

p. xiii: Editorial Review and Outlook "Fruit Frights," *The Wall Street Journal*, March 17, 1989.

p. 3: (Roger Smith writing in *Fortune*), General Motors, Corporate Performance Section, *Fortune*, February 13, 1989, pps. 41–42.

p. 5: Melloan, George, "A Company Held Captive by the Plaintiff Bar," *The Wall Street Journal*, October 4, 1988.

p. 23: Taylor, John, *Storming the Magic Kingdom*, Ballantine Books, New York, 1987, p. 5.

p. 25: Lutz, Adelle et al, "He's Back," *Harper's*, April, 1989.

p. 25: Brown, Patricia Leigh, "Making Over an Image with an Expert's Help," *The New York Times*, January 10, 1989.

p. 27: Packard, Vance, *The Hidden Persuaders* (revised edition), Washington Square Press (Simon & Schuster), : 1957, 1980, p. 28.

p. 60: Bennis, Warren and Burt Nanus, *Leaders: The Strategies for Taking Charge*, Harper & Row, New York, 1985.

p. 78: McCarthy, Michael J., "Sears Plans Blitz of Television Ads Before Christmas," *The Wall Street Journal*, November 2, 1988.

pps. 80–81: Apcar, Leonard M., "A Management Style Passes from Corporate Scene with the Death of Henry Ford II—Last of the Scions," *The Wall Street Journal*, September 30, 1987.

p. 81: Sullivan, Allanna, "Survival Strategy: Texaco's Chiefs Battle to Revitalize the Firm and Repulse Raiders," *The Wall Street Journal*, April 13, 1988.

p. 83: "Big Trouble at Allegheny," *Business Week*, August 11, 1986, p. 58 ff.

p. 84: Shepard, Stephen B., "Editor's Memo," *Business Week*, April 27, 1987, p. 9.

p. 90: Linsky, Martin, *Impact: How the Press Affects Federal Policymaking by Martin Linsky*, W. W. Norton & Company, 1986, p. 61.

p. 114: Ornstein, Norman, Andrew Kohut, and Larry McCarthy: "The People, the Press and Politics."

p. 122: Peters, Tom, *Thriving on Chaos: Handbook for a Management Revolution*, a Borzoi Book. Published by Alfred A. Knopf, Inc., 1987, p. 239.

p. 138: Alsop, Ronald, "Giving Fading Brands a Second Chance," *The Wall Street Journal*, January 24, 1989.

pps. 185–186: Smith, Hedrick, *The Power Game: How Washington Works*, Random House, New York, 1988, p. 404.

p. 223: Miller, William H., "Lobbying's New Arena," *Industry Week*, March 7, 1988, p. 22ff.

p. 240: Kotlowitz, Alex, "Labor's Shift: Finding Strikes Harder to Win, More Unions Turn to Slowdowns." *The Wall Street Journal*, May 22, 1987.

Index

A

Adversary disarray, 119
Agenda, attack on, 127–135
Allegations, false, 72
Announcements
  creating alliances with, 54
  timing of, 54–55
Appeal angle, 115–116
Appeals, emotional, 119–120
Appointments
  announcements of, 54–57
  and the press, 55–56
Associations, 66
  useful, 45–46

Attack
  by acknowledging change
    first, 140
  competitor's farthest lines,
    130
  competitor's home base, 131
  competitor's timing, 132
  from sleeping dog position,
    135
  from smallest defendable
    base, 129
  innovation failures, 134
  loyalty of competitor's allies,
    131
  on narrow front, 129

Attack (*cont.*)
  weakness of leader's strength, 128
  where least expected, 134
  without provoking leader, 130
Authority, clear lines of, 54
Authority endorsements, 124
Awards, 62

B

Being number one, 137–148
  and customer analysis, 139
Big event, 141–142
Breaking with past, 80–81
Bullies, 21–23
Business reading, 87–91

C

Celebrity endorsers, 145–146
  CEO's circle, 43–47
  as recruiting network, 46–47
  and small companies, 46
Ceremonies, 82
Change
  announcement of, 53
  making it an ally, 62
Climate, geography and events, 148
Collaborators, enlistment of, 133
Communication, defined, 8
Community involvements, 67
Controversy, 21
  making use of, 143

Crisis
  power centers, 169
  public interest first, 170
  tell it all and fast, 169
Culture, associating product with, 147
Customers
  commitment to, 78
  making sense to, 114–115
  values, 67–68

D

Defectors, rewards for, 132
Defend
  making adversary spend, 141
  mocking opponent's boldness, 141
  using decoys, 141
Dirty tricks, 69–75
  international, 73
  lies, 74–75
Dress, 27

E

Empowering, 63
Environmentalists 235–238
  affected parties, 237
  authoritative reassurance, 237
  clear messages, 236–237
  get out fast, 238
  hazards, 236
  health and safety risks, 237
Ethics
  communications about, 34
  and conduct codes, 38

and employees, 37
and incentives, 41
and legal behavior, 38–39
standards evident, 36
Etiquette, 27
Execution over ingenuity,
    125–126
Exposure, control of, 72

F

Favor banks, 11–18
Favors
    advertising yours, 16
    authorization for, 14
    build goodwill, 17
    change and, 13–14
    credit rating, 14
    doing them often, 16
    getting credit for, 16
    global, 17–18
    intellectual, 15–16
    you can do, 14
Fearsome reputation, 121
Feelings, 20–21
Fights, picking, 23
Financial crisis
    foe as ally, 157
    old friends for, 156–157
    play for time, 156
    power of nostalgia, 157
    public affairs themes in,
        156
Focus groups, 112–114
    videotaped meetings, 114
Focusing energies, 60–61
Friction, introduction of,
    123–124

G

Gatekeepers, ties to, 145
Geodemography, 110–111
Goals, easy, 134
Government, 217–225
    attitude to business, 225
    be a source, 224–225
    constituencies, 223
    experts, 221
    how people got there, 220
    as lead story, 223–224
    legislative agenda, 223
    staffs, 220–221
    testimony, 221–222
Grapevine, management of, 122

H

History making, 79
Honors, carefully given, 61

I

Image
    consistency, 29–30
    consultants, 25–30
    downscaling, 28–29
Influence, 59–68
    art of, 9
    instead of authority, 65–66
    integrity and, 31–41
    your own, 64–65
Information
    analysis over espionage, 102
    combining, 96–97
    competitor's, 100–101

Information (*cont.*)
  concealing, 103
  from employees, 101
  global, 100
  listening posts, 102
  persuasive, 98
  policy analysis, 103
  protecting informers, 101
  public data, 97
  soft soundings, 104–105
  source for others, 105–106
  study research data, 98–100
Innuendo, 120–121
Integrity and liability, 39–40
Intelligence gathering, 95–106
Interviews
  be alert, 206
  "no comment", 205
  out of context, 208
  outrageous, 207
  photos, 207
  prepare for, 204
  role play, 204–205
  say "No", 205
  taping, 206
  think visually, 206–207
  visual messages, 207

K

Kansas City Hyatt case,
  159–164

L

Labor, 239–242
  communications skills, 240
  ownership and operation, 241

  retired employees, 242
  subtlety, 240
  using employees, 241–242
  women, 241
Leaks, 199–203
  leakers footprints, 202
  pros and cons of, 202–203

M

Management symbolism, 81
Managers, tough and tempera-
  mental, 19–23
Marathon vs. Mobil, 151–157
Maverick, risks of, 84
Media, influence and, 173

N

Nameless number two, 138
Nameless upstart, 138
Needs, yours and theirs, 13
New manager, 51–57
  acting early, 56
  commitments by, 56–57
News, controlling advantage
  of, 122
Nine-digit zip codes, 110

O

"Off the record", 200–201
Opinion surveys, 109
Overpromising, 53

INDEX

P

Parity, maintaining, 66
Persuasion, 124–125
Policy without polling,
    111–112
Power columns, 87–88
Power credentials, 66–67
Power journalists, 88
Power, trappings of, 83
Power triangle, 3–9
Practice your skills, 23
Predecessors
    as symbols, 79
    treatment of, 53
Preferences, 26–27
Press
    economics of, 177
    hostility to business,
        180
    how it shapes opinions,
        177–178
    readers time shortage,
        178–179
    softer attacks, 179
    three levels of, 176–177
    to verify and explain,
        179–180
    trade press, 181–183
Press communications policy,
    202
Press releases, 203
    second opinion, 203–204
Promotion as part of story
    line, 143
Public, win it over and publi-
    cize it, 133
Public relations, essence of,
    246

R

Rainmakers, 12
Reading, non-business,
    90–91
Reporters
    be available, 188
    changing your tactics,
        195–196
    choose your own negatives,
        190
    design your own story, 190
    expect digging, 191
    and the final story,
        194–195
    good news begets bad news,
        191–193
    help them, 188
    high road and company,
        197
    how to sell a story, 189
    and interviews, 186–188
    plan press strategy early,
        195
    respect them, 188
    and the spotlight, 191
    a story a year, 193
    stringing out a story, 195
    and support of others,
        197–198
    sympathy from, 197
    trying to con, 186
    verification of you, 189
Research, 107–116
    unvarnished input, 114
Responsive to needs, 12
Rivalry, being part of,
    146–147
Rumors, 201

INDEX

S

Scene setting, 27–28
Sell the sizzle, 122
Shirt-sleeve thinking, 82
Smarts, 29
Soft villains, 118
Special interests, 227–238
  assign one person, 233
  concessions to, 230
  counterculture methods,
    233–234
  credibility, 229
  environmentalists, 235–238
  eradication of, 231–232
  group splintering, 232
  horse trading, 228–229
  issue and demands, 229–230
  neutral avenues to, 231
  prepare give ups, 230–231
  rallying points of, 232
  risks of winning, 233
  settle early, 230
  think tanks, 234–235
Stature, proper way to show,
  44–45
Story telling, 63–64
Symbolic behavior, 82
Symbolic linkages, 80
Symbol of organization, 85–86

T

Targeting messages, 109–110
Teaching, by action, 78

Telephone calls, verification
  of, 73–74
Television
  audience, 209–210
  business news, 211
  crusading journalism from,
    179
  as entertainment, 209
  live and taped, 210
  media training, 210–211
  message weaving, 213
  proactive video, 212–213
  real audience, 210
  receptive moment, 213–214
  time, 209
Three-Mile Island, 165–170
Tragedy
  compassion in, 163
  loved ones affected, 163
  relief efforts in, 163–164
  use of money in, 163
Trust, 74

U

Unethical behavior, glamorization of, 40–41

V

Victory, declaring, 61
Vocabulary, your own, 121